cogito ergo non opus est machina

I think therefore do not need a machine

©2018 by William Houze
Weather Helm Publications
Arrowsic, Maine
ISBN: 9781729469774

Dedication

To the men and women who want to live their lives free in mind and spirit of the *machine*.

Notable Words

"I would rather have questions that can't be answered than answers that can't be questioned."
--Richard Feynman

"Beyond wisdom there must be foresight. You know that's really the end of the line. Wisdom itself isn't enough. The whole series is data, information, knowledge, wisdom, foresight. There may be something beyond that, but I can't think of it at the moment."
--Arthur C. Clarke

"Humans love all manner of machinery, but humans also love the matrix from which they evolved. We will know that we have succumbed to AI and robotics when we read the *obit* for the Sierra Club, L.L. Bean, and REI—who went the way of the dinosaur because droids were not into Nature like their human creators were."
--Anonymous

Table of Contents

Prolegomena 8
   All the world's a data sea, and you swim in it at your peril 8
      Divergent views: a brief sampling 8
The lecture ploy at the (potentially explosive) C⁵ Gathering 12
The Good Doctor's opening remarks 14
The Cloudy/Digital Zeitgeist 17
   Ideation enumeration 18
      Lead the "digital transformation" 24
      Do *everything* (in IT) faster, faster, faster 25
   Can HR effectively recruit for the Cloud-based and Big Data/AI bound Enterprise? 26
   Final comments on the top 10 strategic imperatives for CIOs/CTOs in 2018 31
   Statements--and questions about statements 35
Root Cause Analysis – Human Progress Before Computers 44
   Pre-Industrial Revolution 45
   Industrial Revolution (c. 1760 – 1860) 46
   Second Industrial Revolution (aka Technological Revolution, c. 1870 - 1914) 46
   Digital Revolution, c. 1947 to present day 46
The old, the simple, the tried-and-proven visual analog processes . 48
Yesterday's paper forms and today's digital forms contain the same information 51
Is data on paper relational—to the human brain? 56

- What Henry Ford can (and should) teach today's CEO 60
- Wheel spoke inventory and production planning: an informative vignette 62

The way IT could be? 65
- What are the options when enveloped in the hyped-fog of expensive ERP, big data, and the cloudscape? 65
- Jim, MIT, the IPC, and ATAP 65
- In the Model T Room 69
- The IPC/ATAP vignette—what does it signify? What is its value? 74
- The paper option = the human (brainiac?) option 76
- Ideal employee profile: high "g" above all else 82
- Occupational complexity and cognitive ability 83
- Annual cost for the back-office digital-free paper enterprise 85
- The low-tech option: the tinker toy ethernet / wireless intranet 86
- Example of On-premise and Cloud Consultant Tasks, Costs, and Timeline 92
- Well, what is next on your agenda? 97
  - 27 radical suggestions for the ("WOKE") CEOs, CFOs, CTOs, CDOs, and their Boards of Directors 97
  - 34 thought points to ponder when putting your feet are up on your desk 101

Closing Thoughts: To Give Way to the Borg, or to Maintain Human Supremacy? 104
- Encouraging Words 120
- Another final word 122

Post-lecture comments 123
- CIO/CDO/CTO comments 123

CEO comments 124
ERP Vendor Comments 125

The Good Doctor, aka the C^5 Lecturer, shortly after receiving his daily jolt of stem-enriched **X^2** soma

Prolegomena

All the world's a data sea, and you swim in it at your peril

Legions of CIOs, CTOs, CDOs, Big Data Wizards, AI-ers, IoT gurus, stealth HR Borgs, and swarms of ERP vendors confront today's beleaguered CEOs. Before the advent of the PC, it was enough to get an A-list MBA, polish your shoes, keep your nose clean, play golf with the right crowd, and presto, your career path was all set. But today's CEO is akin to a member of Odysseus's seafarers who were warned to resist the lure of the Sirens. The Sirens' refrain the CEO hears today is: "listen and reap Golden ROI."

The basic argument is this: financial strength through competitive superiority is only possible if the Enterprise embraces the advantages offered by the cloud, Big Data, AI, IoT. Those who fail to do so will perish.

This eBook "lecture" challenges that assumption by offering several actions the CEO can take to avoid the lure of the Sirens song.

Divergent views: a brief sampling

Pro

"The Cloud and Big Data are here to stay. We must embrace this technology, whatever the cost. The competition will eat our lunch otherwise; we need to move to the very forefront of data

management and Cloud technology. And we need to stay there, no matter what."
(CDO at a major New York City financial institution)

"Interoperability is the *sine qua non* in healthcare. It means everything to us as healthcare providers, and to our patients, it can be the difference between life and death."
(VP and MD, Informatics Officer, major teaching hospital in Los Angeles)

"It is Mission Critical for the United States Armed Forces to have the precise tactical encrypted data it needs, in any location, at any time, under any conditions, and to have it available instantaneously to strategic offensive and defensive platforms on land, sea, and in the air. Today, our National security depends on the proper use and management of weaponized data."
(DARPA, Senior Director R&D, Pentagon)

Con

"When the desktop droid asked, 'Kann ich heute Hilfe leisten?' the young woman pulled its plug, picked up her fountain pen, and resumed writing her first romance novel."
(Anonymous, Berlin)

"If Faust were alive today, he would be churning out Java 2 code at Microsoft or Google—maybe even at Oracle."
(Retired Oracle software engineer, drinking beer at "2-BitJoin," Palo Alto)

"To be free of the infernal machine and its progeny—devil data-- one must live under the sea itself, or in the heart of an active volcano."

(Dr. Anton Anon, an unemployed philosopher living in his van outside of Sausalito)

"I used to be a leader in AI in the Valley; then, after making real money when pioneering AI into integrated business software, my wife convinced me to give it up about the time I was recovering from my first bout with heart disease; so, we bought a small organic farm in Vermont. Now, two years after leaving AI, I feel liberated since I've reconnected to the Earth, something I have not felt since I was an Eagle Scout, but lost around the time I left grad school at Cal Tech. Now I see little value in AI, and I no longer embrace any of the technology like I once did. My eyes have been opened by tending our goats and keeping our bees. All this might sound unbelievable, but it is none the less the one truth I can speak today without hesitation or reservation." A. Kapernik, western Vermont

Undecided/Open Minded/Questioning

"I read something recently that argued against all things Big Tech as being, axiomatically, the future underpinnings of business success in America. When I asked my CIO to read the article and give me her views, she read it and said nothing in tech is black and white. Now what do I do?" CEO of large shipping company, San Pedro, CA.

"Science is never "settled." That is its eternal *sine qua non*. One branch of the tree, technology is likewise transient by definition because of its essential foundational nature. New ideas always emerge to replace the old, so today's tech is soon replaced by tomorrow's. It is an endless progression. But the laws of diminishing returns do apply. And where it is leading you, and what it means to you when you and it arrive together at some future time when you are asked, if not forced, to interact with it, that is the conundrum every executive faces who asks the tough but necessary questions." EVP of Software Engineering R&D firm, Zing Hou, Old Hong Kong

The lecture ploy at the (potentially explosive) C⁵ Gathering

The Scene: You are a member of the disappointingly small audience attending the annual C⁵ (Cloud Conviction and Collaborative Convection Convention) Lecture Series. This means you are surrounded by a smattering of global enterprise-tech groupies and their masters—the handful of assorted C-suiters. You are sitting next to eager adopters of all things smacking of applied code strings. You are one of a hundred or so of confident, often self-appointed **thought-leaders**. But you are unlike them. You are open-minded, and you are there because you want to hear what a well-known, credentialed, but open tech-heretic has to say about all things C⁵.

He is the keynote speaker. He is the Good Doctor invited by the C⁵ organizers who want to employ a bit of reverse psychology by having him posit Position A in the hopes that the audience will reject it out of hand, and instead continue to embrace without reservation Position B. That is, to continue to march to the drum beat of those who embrace everything that C⁵ implies.

Knowing all this, you watch as the Key Note speaker walks to the podium, clicks his clicker, and then you see following on the twelve foot Cisco Spark screen:

The 2018 C⁵ Lecture Series

The Question:

"Are ERP, Big Data, and AI/Machine Learning Necessary and Good in the Human Workplace?"

The Answer:

cogito ergo no opus est machina

I think therefore do not need a machine

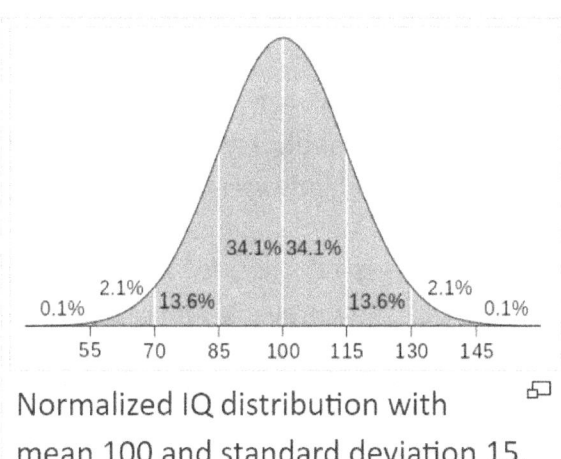

Normalized IQ distribution with mean 100 and standard deviation 15.

https://en.wikipedia.org/wiki/Intelligence_quotient

The Good Doctor's opening remarks

"Ladies and Gentlemen, I am by training first a scientist, and by no training at all, also a philosopher poet. One the one hand, I inhabit a world where my thoughts and conclusions are based on logic and the unyielding constraints of Empiricism. And on the other, I spend time in the shower thinking like a philosopher, or in a hammock dreaming like a poet, which means I delve into realms beyond those usually habituated by an empiricist. In short, I am someone who uses the mind, the intellect, the reason to explore thoughts, feelings, ideas, and impulses that properly speaking fall both within and without the boundaries of the scientific method in the strict definition of that concept when put into practice.

We follow the scientific method that originated with the Chinese, Greeks, Babylonians, and Egyptians. Occasionally we have hunches (Einstein had many of them, fortunately) that we subject to the rigor of scientific experimentation, analysis of repeatable and independently verifiable results. Eventually this process leads us to reasoned statements and demonstrations of a given cause and effect—to Laws--of what man is able to know as being true because it is provable and repeatable on any given day here on Earth, on Mars, wherever Stephen Hawking wants to place us.

But first and last, we rely on our ability to think, to reason, to assess data before us and to arrive at sound conclusions—the very essence of the scientific method handed down to us by men and women who, without hesitation, functioned first as thinking humans, using "tools" as needed to get the work at hand done.

This very bedrock notion—our ability to think independently of tools, a.k.a, machines, --is expressed in the Latin phrase: *cogito ergo non opus est machina (I think therefore do not need a machine)*.

The plain meaning in this Latin phrase has been the method followed by such luminaries as Pythagoras, Newton, Leibnitz, and by the pioneers of machine computation and machine instruction language, from Babbage and Lovelace early on down to Turing—a body of human thought that eventually gave us today's laptop, tablet, cell phone, and smart wrist watch.

Based on that factual foundation and observation of phenomena, we refrain from the impulse to extrapolate, and when we do, we couch such musing as hypotheses that we subject to the methodology of science. The outcome is eventually binary: the results and findings are repeatable and are again and again verified to be the expected outcome by many observers.

There is no middle ground except for Heisenberg's Uncertainty Principle, but that is another matter altogether in the realm of quantum physics and need not concern us here in the realm of ERP, Big and Small Data, AI, and the hot new ideas making up the buzz around so-called Machine Learning[1].

---

[1] "Azure Machine Learning, Open and elastic AI development spanning the cloud and the edge" See, https://azure.microsoft.com/en-us/overview/machine-learning/. The site offers this marketing definition of Machine Learning: "Machine learning enables computers to learn from data and experiences and to act without being explicitly programmed. Customers can build Artificial Intelligence (AI) applications that intelligently sense, process, and act on information - augmenting human capabilities, increasing speed and efficiency, and helping organizations achieve more."

Why, you might ask, should any of this scientific method matter to you, the Executives of the Enterprise, who were in our grandfather's time called the Captains of Industry?

The Thesis: I am arguing that before you continue your journey to embrace the latest and greatest apps in the ERP Cloud and the data in it, that each of you should ask yourself a series of key questions that are designed to test and challenge your assumptions before you make costly decisions about Big ERP, Big Data, AI, and the rest of it. And this should concern you whether you run a hospital, a university, an insurance company, or a manufacturing plant in China producing iPhones and MacBooks from a sea of parts sourced and made as cheaply as possible world-wide.

So, let me present you with current-state situation statements and pose some questions to test your readiness to accept as dogma the latest marketing line pushed by Big Tech.

If you like, you can think of what I am presenting as propositions that are intended to make you think; that are designed to give you pause before committing to a path that takes you into a land of no easy return—or perhaps, of no return at all.

The Cloudy/Digital Zeitgeist

There are so many buzz words alive and well today about all things ERP and Big Data that one is hard pressed to keep up with the latest jargon buzzing around the Web like Fly Bots. (A jargon filter is mandatory!) Some of the major buzz-products and related services alive and well today include these well-known concepts/products: Cloud, Cloudlets, PaaS, IaaS, SaaS, IoT, Big ERP, Big Data, AI, Machine Learning, et al.

Here is a drastically simplified look at the concepts behind the technology stack and the elements in the Cloud atmospherics. First, the "Cloud Stack" showing the relationship between the User Earthling and the facilitators who make apps and data available to them via the internet:

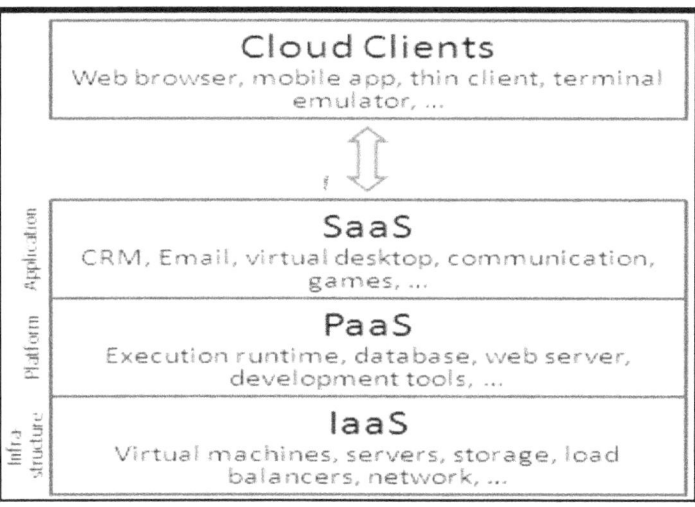

[2] Generic overview of the Cloud service models

---

[2] See, https://en.wikipedia.org/wiki/Cloud_computing

The generic image below shows the interrelationship of the basic components that are found in a typical Cloud Computing platform[3]:

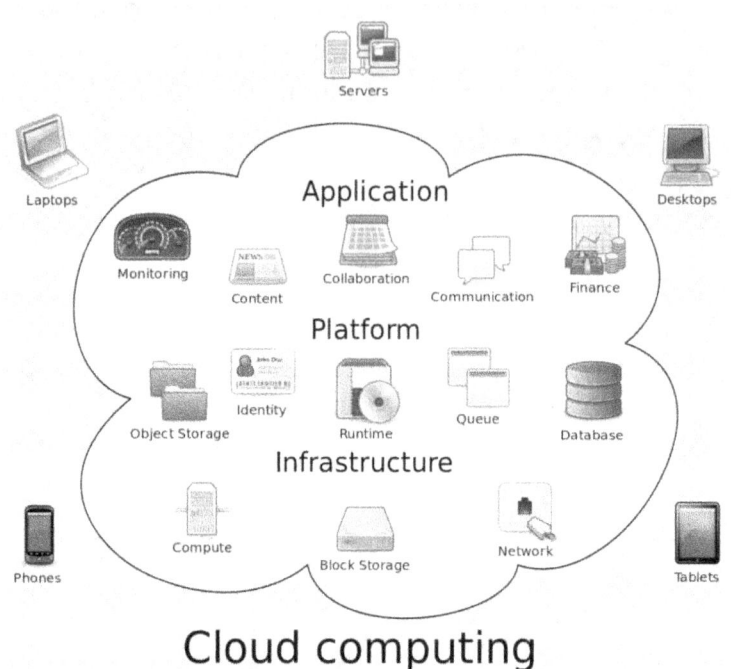

Ideation enumeration

For the latest in technology trends in 2018 in the ERP mega-industry, Gartner summarizes the coming trends:

"The intelligent digital mesh is a foundation for future digital business and its ecosystems. To create competitive advantage,

---

[3] See, https://en.wikipedia.org/wiki/Cloud_computing

enterprise architecture and technology innovation leaders must evaluate these top trends to identify opportunities that their organizations can exploit.[4]

And here is the list of coming trends that Gartner covers in its article:

Trend No. 1: AI Foundation
Today's AI Is Narrow AI
Trend No. 2: Intelligent Apps and Analytics
Augmented Analytics Will Enable Users to Spend More Time Acting on Insights
Trend No. 3: Intelligent Things
Swarms of Intelligent Things Will Work Together
Trend No. 4: Digital Twins
Digital Twins Will Be Linked to Other Digital Entities
Trend No. 5: Cloud to the Edge
Edge Computing Brings Distributed Computing into the Cloud Style
Trend No. 6: Conversational Platforms
Integration with Third-Party Services Will Further Increase Usefulness
Trend No. 7: Immersive Experience
VR and AR Can Help Increase Productivity
Trend No. 8: Blockchain
Blockchain Offers Significant Potential Long-Term Benefits Despite Its Challenges
Trend No. 9: Event-Driven Model
Events Will Become More Important in the Intelligent Digital Mesh
Trend No. 10: Continuous Adaptive Risk and Trust

---

[4] See, https://www.gartner.com/doc/3811368?srcId=1-6595640781

Barriers Must Come Down Between Security and Application Teams

As for the forecasted state of IT in 2018, another source, Spiceworks, indicates:

"Currently, 29% of organizations have adopted IoT, 18% have adopted VR, and 13% have adopted AI. And adoption is expected to grow significantly in the next 12 months. An additional 19% of organizations plan to adopt IoT next year while another 14% and 17% plan to adopt VR and AI, respectively.

Adoption of emerging tech trends is even higher in larger organizations. In fact, about 30% of organizations with 1,000+ employees say they've adopted AI, and an additional 25% plan to adopt it next year. Perhaps the rise in IT budgets is leading more companies to jump on the latest trends."[5]

IT budgets indeed appear to be on the increase, given that ERP vendors are projected to rake in more than $40B by 2020. The factors contributing to this marketing-driven bonanza for Big ERP/Cloud vendors (like SAP, Oracle, Infor, Microsoft, NETSUITE) are many.

Here are just six of many, many reasons why ERP vendors are thriving:

1. Once big business left the tried and true paper system for the allure of Moore's Law and the promise of ever-increasing efficiency and exponential collaboration via networked computers, printers, and data bases, there was no one willing to put the Digital Genie back in the office clerk's ink bottle;

---

[5] See, https://www.spiceworks.com/marketing/state-of-it/report/

2. CIOs and CTOs are poorly equipped (by training, education, and because most of them today in positions of power came of age with Apple) to give serious thought to comparing alternative system costs and efficiencies against what they believed were at hand via Big ERP;
3. Most C-Suiters rely on and therefore eventually buy in to what their CIOs and CTOs recommend as being required to succeed in the competitive marketplace—a Cloud-based, on-premise, or hybrid-based ERP system;
4. The persuasive power of marketing hype and vendor demos (e.g., nuanced integrated applications, dynamic on-screen report generation, dashboard alerts, and situational analytics) pushed by sales and self-appointed "value engineers;"
5. Fear of becoming non-competitive if not on the latest ERP back-office system offering near-real-time cube-based data analytics, "what-if" scenario modeling, increased power and scaling to handle future system demands, and big data storage and retrieval;
6. The allure of positive ROI based on the promise that Cloud-based ERP delivery models (IaaS, PaaS, SaaS, IoT, AI, Machine Learning) translate into lower IT staffing costs, increased processing efficiencies, and reduced back-office staffing needs across the enterprise.

Here are seven reasons, all of them rather obvious it would seem, why CIOs are so wed to ERP systems[6]:

1. Saving money

---

[6] See SelectHub, https://selecthub.com/enterprise-resource-planning/why-erp-systems-are-important/

2. Improved collaboration
3. Better analytics
4. Improved productivity
5. Happier customers
6. Simplified regulatory compliance
7. Improved inventory and production management

Of course, the ERP vendors push this line of reasoning in the sales cycle. It is difficult to imagine today's CIOs/CTOs dismissing the sales pitch out of hand. They are, it seems, locked into the ERP Cloud paradigm; given the projected growth of ERP via the Cloud, it appears CIOs/CTOs have little if any inclination (intellectual ability?) to question the potential repercussions of giving in to the intellectual and emotional fog that leads them into THE CLOUD in the first place.

Consider this dose of the myriad competing pressures on CIOs as summarized by Forbes *BrandVoice*:

"More so than in any other year in recent history, events in 2017 promise to put business executives under intense pressure, as new political forces, restructured trading coalitions, and more aggressive central bankers and regulators exert their influence on companies and markets worldwide.

Advances in digital technology and business models will also continue to shift the balance of global economic power, putting more pressure on CIOs to stay ahead of existing and emerging competitors. The many tools at the disposal of CIOs include cloud computing, predictive analytics, mobile applications, machine learning, and robotics, feeding broader movements such as the Internet of Things and Industry 4.0. The business opportunities are considerable: lower costs; more precise supply chains; more dynamic, reliable, and personalized products and marketing campaigns; more attentive customer service; and ultimately more abundant, loyal customers."[7]

Considering this reality facing the CIO, Forbes came up with the top ten strategic priorities the CIO must address in 2017 to remain competitive[8]:

1. Lead your company's digital transformation, don't just facilitate it.
2. Stop just talking about "customer-centricity" and the "customer experience" and start living it.
3. Put software and data analytics at the center of your company: the IoT challenge.
4. Do *everything* faster.
5. Give your developers the gift of agility.
6. Recommit to the most important IT acronym: HR.
7. Put what data you can in the cloud—to *shore up* security.
8. Start closing or consolidating your own data centers.
9. Figure out what artificial intelligence can do for your company and organization.
10. Finally lay out a plan for escaping the 80/20 trap.

This list of priorities is based on a series of assumptions about what is best for the Enterprise, and many of them are exactly

---

[7] See, https://www.forbes.com/sites/oracle/2017/01/17/top-10-strategic-cio-priorities-of-2017/#275bd8154e42

[8] See, https://www.forbes.com/sites/oracle/2017/01/17/top-10-strategic-cio-priorities-of-2017/#4216db9c4e42

what will merely add to the chaos surrounding the headlong rush to expand the digitized enterprise. A few comments about some of the items in the list are in order.

Lead the "digital transformation"

Leading a "digital transformation" assumes the CIO/CTO will have the factual basis, the background knowledge, and the sound and impartial judgement required to set a viable course of action in the digital realm.

Considering that the information available is rife with marketing wishful thinking, not to mention "idea landmines" born of digital daydreaming by software engineers and self-anointed "thought leaders" in the "industry" who are paid to come up the "something new and better on a daily basis," it would be nearly impossible to assemble a valid set of facts and then assess them on their merits.

How would the CIO/CTO be able to arrive at, and then separate the pie in the sky from the impartial case studies, from the empirical evidence? And where does one go to find reliable empirical evidence? Who has assembled it, and if they have, who are they? What are their basic assumptions? What is their understanding of the pros and cons informing the movement towards transforming much of life in pursuit of the "digital realm?"

The assumption is that your average CIO/CTO can lead the enterprise to digital transformation based on the pertinent the facts upon which to weigh the pros and cons. If this were the case, the 70% failure rate of major digital initiatives (IT projects) would be much lower than the historical record indicates.[9]

Do everything (in IT) faster, faster, faster

In my view, the very notion that everything must be done faster along the High Tech Highway is about as empty-headed an idea as one can imagine. Speed kills on the highway full of cars and on the digital highway full of projects that are either driverless (poor project management and uninformed and/or insufficient executive oversight) or are moving forward towards a destination that is not worth the price paid to get there. Think of a fiscal cliff, perhaps.

The assumption, of course, is that the fast-moving firm across town will be early adopters of the latest technology (insert the system or field of your choice) and as a result will rob the sluggish enterprise of its customers, market share, and dividend payout; that their use of technology will give the competitors such a strategic advantage that it will be impossible to catch up, that once behind, there is no way to catch up.

The fallacy in this line of thinking is that given the cookie-cutter nature of today's ERP systems, incremental improvements offered in one ERP system over another do not matter all that much in terms of operational advantage ; or that being in the Cloud before your next competitor arrives there will translate into operational advantages, or that Big Data calls and puts efficiencies across the workforce translate into better or more

---

[9] See, http://www.reply-mc.com/2010/09/19/why-70-of-changes-fail-by-rick-maurer/

timely decision-making; or that a tighter integration between the company and the customer base will translate into new customers or more loyal customers.

Can HR effectively recruit for the Cloud-based and Big Data/AI bound Enterprise?

The HR department cannot be the savior of IT executives who are desperate to bring on the qualified staff they need to run an ever-more esoteric digital system. If it is Cloud based, then the enterprise becomes a "thin client" in many respects. System analysis, maintenance, patch management (for apps, environment, database, security, and access auditing) all fall to the remote host/provider. In this regard, the IT staff needs are few compared to the old on premise setup.

And in the Cloud multi-tenancy schema, the customer has very limited access to the system, the data, and certainly none to the security setup. ERP system admin support by employees in house is no longer one of the major concerns of the CIO. The more the Cloud becomes the apps and data delivery model for the customer base, the less the CIO will ask HR to recruit ERP support talent.

Of course, the downside to this scenario is that support is often offshore, and that gets into issues of time zones, language barriers, and therefore responsiveness to customer system operational needs. On line and functioning as intended SLAs of 99.5% or higher might be what Cloud marketing and sales promise.

They will even provide "statistical proof" of uptime for their Cloud multi- and solo tenants. But there are many points of failure between the surgical supply's buyer at the keyboard in the hospital and the millennial techies sitting in their cubes in Panama, Manilla, or Bombay. Offshore Cloud support failure does occur, and it can bring hell into the lives of CIOs/CTOs and HR VPs.

A case in point is the "well-known" Microsoft Azure Cloud failure:

> "Operator error was the root cause of the catastrophic failure of Microsoft's Azure cloud computing platform on 19 November 2014, which left many customers unable to access the service. . . . While public cloud operators will argue they experience far less downtime than in-house IT, given the scale of Microsoft and Amazon Web Services (AWS), any hitch impacts millions of people. The Azure service was not fully operational for more than 11 hours. Being without a basic utility like gas, electricity or water for 11 hours would be classed as a major incident – for an e-commerce website, the cost of downtime amounts to millions of [pounds] in lost revenue."[10]

All this means that executives who rely on the Cloud, and a body of unknown support staff located who knows where and with what skills, are at the mercy of the vendor to meet system online SLAs by contract, and to ensure data is not breached by anyone for any reason.

But it also means these same executives are at the mercy of their HR departments to find the kind of staff they will need to provide emergency workarounds when the Cloud and the data in it fails the enterprise. The same executives will also need HR to provide them with the resources needed to make sense of the kind of analytics the Cloud vendors will push out to the enterprise. These same scarce resources will also have to help the executives understand and make decisions based on the data

---

[10] See, http://www.computerweekly.com/news/2240235106/Operator-error-the-root-cause-of-Microsoft-Azure-failure

pushed out in the form of analytical presentation to their smart watches, cell phones, and smart pads. Can the HR staff find and qualify such resources that that the execs will have to rely on to get and understand their enterprise "data news" and "key data trends" impacting established KPIs.

Where, then does this leave the HR department in its role to support the enterprise by bringing on the kind of talent needed if the ERP system is totally Cloud based? Here is what a contributor to *The Harvard Business Review* has to say on the notion that HR needs to be transformed itself to support the enterprise in the age of Big Data, AI, and all things Cloud.

Ram Charan, writing in the *Harvard Business Review*, argues it is time to split the traditional HR department/staff into two different functional groups. He writes:

"I talk with CEOs across the globe who are disappointed in their HR people. They would like to be able to use their chief human resource officers (CHROs) the way they use their CFOs—as sounding boards and trusted partners—and rely on their skills in linking people and numbers to diagnose weaknesses and strengths in the organization, find the right fit between employees and jobs, and advise on the talent implications of the company's strategy. . . .. My proposal is to eliminate the position of CHRO and split HR into two strands. One—we might call it HR-A (for administration)—would primarily manage compensation and benefits. It would report to the CFO, who would have to see compensation as a talent magnet, not just a major cost. The other, HR-LO (for leadership and organization), would focus on improving the people capabilities of the business and would report to the CEO."[11]

Charan's point is right on the money, in my view. HR must morph into agents capable of playing the role of strategic advisors. This is especially important when it comes to finding the right talent to help the enterprise's leadership understand the ins and outs of all things AI, Big Data, Machine Learning, et al. Of course, this means HR will have to recruit and qualify the data scientists and others of that ilk who can translate the output of the Cloud into understandable information for those expected by their Boards to make the right decisions based on the right information at the right time.

Understanding IBM's Data Life Cycle shown below illustrates what HR will have to understand in concept and application when looking for the resources needed in the Brave New World of Big Data/AI.[12]

---

[11] See, "It's time to split HR," July-August, 2014, *Harvard Business Review*, https://hbr.org/2014/07/its-time-to-split-hr

[12] See IBMs "Team Data Science Process Documentation," https://docs.microsoft.com/en-us/azure/machine-learning/team-data-science-process/

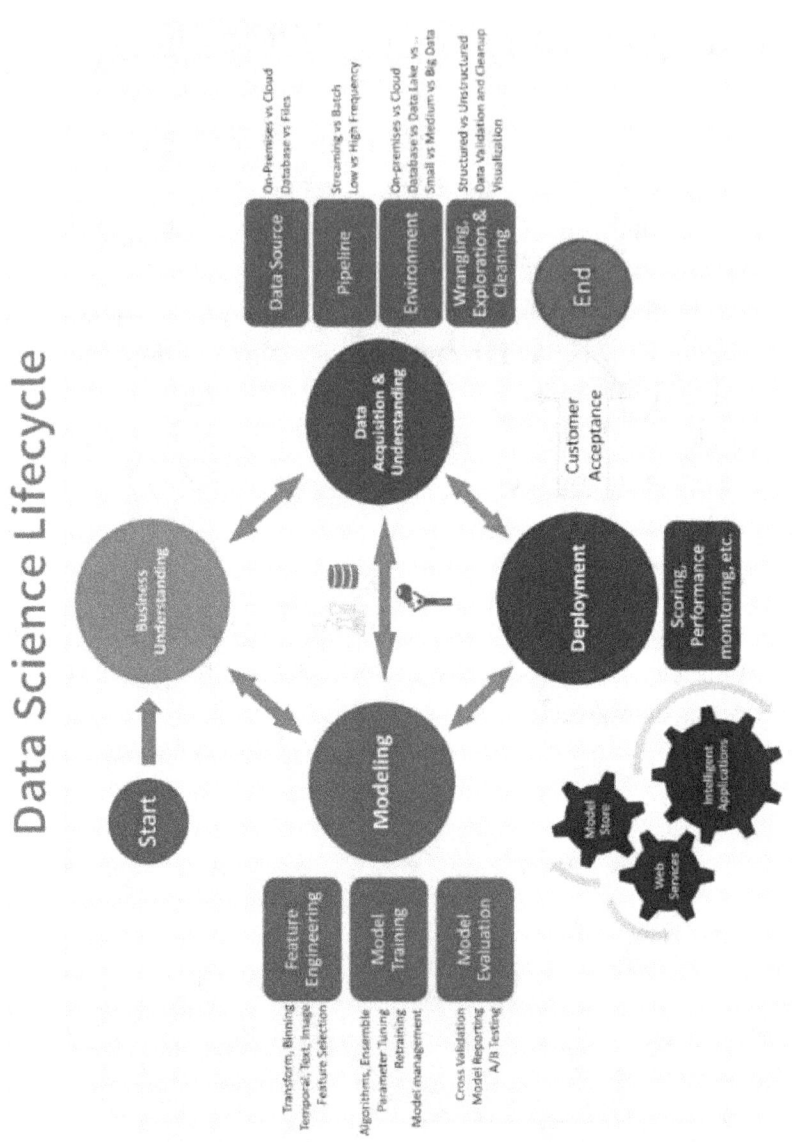

This graphic illustrates the complexity of the task facing HR—from grasping the basics of the data lifecycle process to finding and validating resources who are deep into data science. Failing to so this in the near term, or at all, does not bode well for enterprise leadership who have "gone all in," as the poker saying goes in Vegas, on the hand Cloud hawking vendors have dealt them.

And please permit me to offer you one more observation about the inability of most everyone in the Enterprise to ascertain who is and is not qualified to sever as a top Data expert. For it should be obvious to you, as it is to me, that beyond HR being unable to intelligently determine the qualifications of the kind of guru who would manage the "data life cycle" for the Enterprise, one can also throw in executives outside of IT, and more likely than not, many within IT as well. None of them really have a clue, in my opinion, and those who claim they do are not looking for a slot in the machinery of the Enterprise. They already have a gig in hand: Cal Tech, MIT, or other places where they prostrate themselves before the "Godata."

Final comments on the top 10 strategic imperatives for CIOs/CTOs in 2018

The strategic objectives 7 through 10 could well occasion a mixture of outright laughter and a severe state of incredulity. At least that is my assessment.

To shore up security for data by placing it in the Cloud is preposterous on the face of it. Cloud security breaches are on the increase. The more data there is in the Cloud schema, the greater the richness of the target becomes for all who will seek and find ways to penetrate the all conceivable barriers. "Vulnerabilities in shared technology pose a significant threat to cloud computing. Cloud service providers share infrastructure, platforms, and applications, and if a vulnerability arises in any of these layers, it affects everyone."[13]

Closing or consolidating data centers on-premise simply moves it to the Cloud or consolidates it. In either case, the threat level remains real. It is only a matter of time until the weak points manifest themselves and the door is opened. The result can be fines, loss of customers, and in the case of privileged data (classified and medical, for example), the legal repercussions can be significant.

And the RCA, or root cause analysis, of cyber security risk from hackers clearly goes beyond "code writer blinders" to the very design of Intel's chip logic itself. In January of 2018, the prospect of Intel chip design flaws, and the vulnerability to hackers accessing data and passwords, came to light in a report in the Wall Street Journal.[14]

In this article, the author sums up this fundamental threat (Google Jann Horn, the young German researcher who first alerted Intel to the flaw in the chip design in their own chips released over the last ten years) to those who rely more and more on the computer and its data children to operate in today's commercial environment:

 ". . . patches and other software fixes may not be the definitive answer. Patches can protect against Meltdown. But it isn't clear if they can fully protect against Spectre. CERT, a federally funded

---

[13] See, https://www.infoworld.com/article/3041078/security/the-dirty-dozen-12-cloud-security-threats.html

[14] See, https://www.wsj.com/articles/businesses-rush-to-contain-fallout-from-major-chip-flaws-1515160803

cybersecurity research organization at Carnegie Mellon University, initially said on Wednesday that only new hardware could fully fix it. But . . ., <u>it updated its assessment</u>, saying updates to operating systems or apps could "mitigate these attacks."

Still, experts say full protection might require design changes, which could take a year to roll out. Luckily, they experts say Spectre is a difficult attack to mount. It requires tailoring to the systems being targeted, and hackers might take a while before figuring out how to take advantage."

Perhaps the most ridiculous strategic goal for the CIO/CTO in 2017 was to suggest they will have the wherewithal to figure out how AI can play a positive and productive role in the enterprise. One can only imagine the feeble attempts they will make as they attempt to understand the role of AI in the workplace, study examples of where AI is making a positive difference in terms of efficiency, productivity, collaboration across employees, so forth.

The AI jargon alone and its applications in various work scenarios will consume months of careful study and parsing by the IT executives and their staffs. Then what? How will AI be integrated? Who will install and manage AI? Who will measure AI in terms of productivity, ROI, so forth? What will the displaced or otherwise impacted employees have to say about AI in their midst? And if the AI is internal to the software and/or to the servers in the Cloud, how will that give one enterprise an advantage over the others who will also have access to the same

AI applications? (For a high-level review of AI in workplace, see *Datamation*, "Pros and Cons of Artificial Intelligence".[15])

Finally, CIOs are seeking ways to stop spending 80% of their budgets on IT staff requirements on-premise so they can spend more than the remaining 20% available for productive "Imagineering." Going to the Cloud negates having to pay for an on-premise IT staff of the same skill sets and size when the systems were housed onsite.

But much of that money is earmarked for the Cloud SaaS subscription and support fees. So, the ratio might be more like 40/60 if they are in the Cloud. But one wonders what the 60% will be used for once the enterprise data and systems are Cloud-based? And whatever it is used for, will the CIO be able to demonstrate ROI as an outcome?

Let me summarize. The likelihood that the average CIO will be able to achieve these strategic goals in any significant measure in 2017, or in the foreseeable future, is slim to none. They are no more able to shape their digital destiny today than they were at the advent of the computer age.

Like their counterparts in the C-Suite, they are constrained by one or more of the following realities confronting them daily:

- Inability to escape the clutches of CIO/CTO Group Think
- Fear of being rejected by fellow executives if they do not embrace the latest tech trends

---

[15] See, https://www.datamation.com/applications/pros-and-cons-of-artificial-intelligence.html

- High cost for Big ERP (fees, security, consultants, support, maintenance, licensing, training, organizational change management, the list goes on and on)
- Failure take sufficient time to explore alternatives in depth before making key decisions
- Egoism and the certainty that they know what is needed blinds them of their imperfect and fragmented knowledge of viable options
- Scarce resources needed to put "the strategic plan" into action, support and maintain it
- Inability (or unwillingness) to capitalize on lessons learned from past ERP boondoggles
- Resistance across the Enterprise for trying anything that is radically new and different

Statements--and questions about statements

Cloud/ERP Statement: Big ERP is predicted to be a $40B industry by 2020[16], which means that Executives around the world agree that this path forward (using PaaS, IaaS, or SaaS platforms for Big ERP and Big Data) is correct, is the best of all possible paths to take. Otherwise, the trend to embrace all things-Cloud would make it impossible to even project such a trend.

Questions: I ask you, have you read and analyzed case studies *conducted by impartial observers*—not vendors--that show the trend to the Cloud is grounded in sound predictive statistical

---

[16] See, http://www.erpnews.com/erp-market-size-expected-exceed-49-billion-2020/

method? What is the basis for the projected growth? Has the Cloud become the best place to achieve significant and measurable financial advantages? Is it secure enough to offset the risk of being hacked, taken hostage, or falling prey to inevitable operator errors, or virus infection that attacks all online and backed up data produced out of the ERP software platform?

Data Statement: There are fundamental problems associated with interpreting what data means. Raw data is not the same thing as structured information. And there is a difference between "nature's or the universe's raw data" and "system generated raw data" that is placed in relational databases—or tables.

You need to understand what the difference is, what it means, and the limited uses of structured data. And if a neural AI machine helps interpret what the machine or system data means,[17] that will not remove the basic problems for humans trying to understand what the Big Machine-System data means as well.

This is because machine-generated data (running on a computer language that enables the machine to execute specific commands) is a product of people processes that underlie the software itself; you can think of it as anthropomorphic-centric data put into and generated out of ERP software processes. This data is not the same as phenomena observable in the Natural World (measuring gravity produces one very different kind of data from that which comes out of an ERP financial engine.)

---

[17] See, https://www.kdnuggets.com/2015/10/data-science-machine.html

The human forces (micro- and macro-economics, politics, the unconscious mind impacting the conscious rational mind) governing the input into ERP systems are not at all the same forces that are today detectable and quantifiable even in the inductive/deductive realm of particle physics. I invite you to think long and hard about the implications of what I have just said.

Questions: Do you know what the qualifications should be for a Chief Data Officer (CDO)? For a "data scientist?" How will you, or the HR department hiring staff, know how to determine if the CDO should be up to the latest research like that behind the "Data Science Machine"[18] at MIT? Who will know what to ask the potential CDO, the data scientist?

Is the data generated by the ERP system understandable to the extent you can make valid decisions based on the financial and operational trends it shows you? How reliable are the pattern analyses out of Big Data that Machine Learning promises to produce in ever-more-sophisticated predictive analytics? Will your CDO understand this, and will you understand it when the CDO shows it to you? How do you decide what to trust and what not to trust? Is it an "either/or" proposition in all cases?

Do you know what the limits of meaningful data mining are? What about the meaning of even simple data presentations which have underlying complex assumptions and conditions (the governing data context of perhaps thousands of variables) that

---

[18] See Mayo's write up on Kanter's & Veeramachaneni's "Data Science Machine" in: https://www.kdnuggets.com/2015/10/data-science-machine.html

are outside of but bearing directly or indirectly upon the ERP system that produced the data?

Does any data in any context--no matter how well it is selected, presented, and analyzed-- offer you sound empirical analytics that enable the most reason-based yet flexible strategic business decisions?[19] Does the CDO, or do you yourself, know the ins and outs of data phenomena, of basic tenets of data epistemology?

Does someone working for you understand the complexities and uncertainties of all data, and do you trust their judgment? Do you understand these matters yourself? Should you? Is Cloud ERP best for your employees who must use it daily? Have you personally, along with and your employee "experts," observed first-hand how pure or hybrid Cloud ERP systems meet the needs of another enterprise in your line of business? Is this inside look possible?

 Should you insist that it be done upfront by you and your team of technology and business "experts?"

Client-Server, On-Premise Statement: There is no definable strategic advantage of returning to a well-designed and expertly supported on-premise client-server system (LAN/WAN) over the latest pure or hybrid Cloud model. Doing so will likely mean the enterprise falls behind its competitors because it will be less

---

[19] "There is much debate on this topic. The view that data analytics serve as a sound decision-making basis depends always on the validity of the data itself; but far more critical is the ability to understand what the tea leaves reveal, then putting into practice actions in the business realm based on those readings. This entire process is subject to errors large and small." Dr. W. Houze, retired ERP consultant.

collaborative, less integrated, less data-centric, and less externally focused and internet based.

Questions: Have you conducted a thorough, rigorous, and objective fact-based cost-benefit analysis of the client-server, on-premise model costs, security, risks, and complexity of maintaining and supporting compared to the cost for PaaS, IaaS, SaaS models and their associated mixtures of risk, support, and maintainability by offshore millennials just out of school, or undergoing OJT?

Are you prepared to rely on AI or smart machines to manage the health of your database? To automatically scale up for memory and processor power when you acquire another company and it directly impacts your requirements for "ping, power, and pipe?"

Have you looked at the pros and cons of entirely cloud-based or a hybrid setup where some hardware runs software on-premise, but other key elements are hosted remotely, e.g., primary transactional database and its off-line "high-available" backed-up database?

Off the Shelf Hardware and Customizable Software On-Premise

Statement: There is no way one can cost-effectively run a major enterprise on networked (LAN/WAN) laptops, printers, fax machines, office phones from Best Buy, Quick Books Enterprise, Excel, or from a home-brewed integrated suite of business processes based on commercially available "business process forms" that can be used out of the box; or that consultant developers can customize or create out of base code(Java?) to do exactly what the business users need the system to do for them in finance, payroll, supply chain management, HR, shop floor control, production planning, so forth.

Questions: Have you taken the time to develop a cost-benefit study based on the easily obtained (search online at Amazon, Best Buy, Office Max) hardware and OTS software costs for the basics of the system you need to support your back-office business processes, doing ONLY what is essential to run the business and meet all external regulatory compliance rules and laws in Finance, HR, and ISO quality control measures in manufacturing industries?

Have you looked at Microsoft, for example, and the cost of subscribing to Office 365 on a corporate level, including options for storing data onsite?

Do you really think the current staffing levels across corporate America in 2018 are justifiable? How many executives are really needed to manage the business? Can you imagine a situation where capable employees of above average intelligence are able to use OTS software and generic laptops to run the entire human resources (formerly personnel) department?

Or must you have a VP, assistant VPs, Directors, and Managers, and Leads to handle the basics of human resources, employee benefits, compliance with state and federal regulations, and so forth? (By now, I think you know where I stand on this one!)

Now, this is one set of questions about one department in the organization. There are others you can ask as well across the enterprise from an organizational, cost, and efficiency perspective. So, examine the continuum with the balance sheet in mind, as well as keeping in mind what is best for people who spend their lives "at work."

The Totally Digital-free ERP System Statement: To revert to the pen, pencil, the file cabinet, the rolodex, the paper office forms, the written general ledger and chart of accounts, the long list supply item master, paper bills and invoices, paper checks for payroll and paying the bills—there is no way any business should revert to what was used before the advent of the computer in the back-office environment.

Questions: All of you will dismiss out of hand the option of using a digital-free, software-free, database-free system in today's enterprise world that rests on three pillars: Computer processors, integrated business processing software, and relational database schemas. Here is what you believe.

Without these basics in the enterprise, you would be thrown back into the "lattice-work" of the Dark Ages. You would be left helpless before the vicissitudes of an army of file clerks, paper shufflers, pen pushers, ink blotters users, ink pad hand stamps, memos on bulletin boards, in baskets piled high with paper to read and process.

What about those sallow-complexioned people who wear green visors on their heads bent low over massive tomes in which they write serried arrays of numbers, words, and shorthand notations? Remember them? You would be locked out of the Digital Age.[20]

But if you were, you would be in some rather accomplished company from the past. Consider the achievements of Edison Power and Light, AT&T, US Steel, or the Ford Motor Company accomplished, and even the writing of the Declaration of Independence, the US Constitution, the Bill of Rights.

---

[20] See, https://www.techopedia.com/definition/23371/digital-revolution

Consider that everything was done at a much slower pace, that they accomplished much without the digitized computer, without your Cloud hosted business processing software, and the latest Oracle or Microsoft database release. Could you organize your enterprise, your workforce, to do as well as what was accomplished by Egyptian Pharaoh's employing clerks writing on papyrus?

Could you manage what these people did? For example, consider: the recorded legal opinions of Roman lawyers, the intricate checks and balances used by German bankers, the detailed screeds and sacred records kept by the Vatican, the organizers of the great library in Alexandria, the low-tech production techniques put into place English textile mill managers?

The answer is that of course you could—if you thought it was worth doing, if you figured out how to balance some losses in business processing efficiency in the back office for major cost savings.

Imagine Enterprise Central Processing that is integrated, that is the nexus of the enterprise operations center. It consists of at most ten people in the central processing room, using laptops from Best Buy to process business transactions across the enterprise by using Excel, Quick Books, Access DB, producing reports, backing up the database, releasing orders via fax for supplies, running payroll via OTS system. Their laptops are connected via intranet, they can share files, data, reports, and business process forms. They use the fax machine to order supplies.

In summary, here are the key ideas in this last option: keep it all in house, keep it simple, keep it low-tech, use software OTS, use Excel, Access DB, so forth. Stress business strategy and basic data analytics; stress creativity and collaboration; eschew the internet, the Cloud, all the models of remote back office software for a fee; consider balance between efficiency, accuracy, security, cost, and favoring people over AI, over S/W when people can do it better.

Now I know many of you, perhaps all of you, are less than enthused by what I have said thus far. And that is understandable. After all, you have not been exposed to options based on ideas outside of what your average CIO, CTO, CDO are going to present to you. That is because they too are locked into a narrow range of thought, into what the latest "white papers" convey to them about the latest research, the hottest ideas pushed by sophisticated marketing departments leading the charge in all of the major ERP system providers.

But you need to take a long look at all options. You need to understand what human intelligence can do in running the Enterprise.

Let us review what people have accomplished, and I am speaking of people with average, above average, and very high levels of intelligence have accomplished down through the ages. In brief, what IQ coupled with high-energy, attention to detail, and the ability to focus on and accomplish mundane tasks as well as very difficult tasks have given us down through the ages.

Root Cause Analysis – Human Progress Before Computers

We know that human intelligence, not blind luck or divine intervention, has made it possible for mankind to not only survive but to achieve so much in so many areas of endeavor. At the risk of stating the obvious, permit me to point out that high human intelligence is why we have so many wondrous inventions and progress, all of which has been to the benefit of mankind.

It is also true, of course, the human brain has also brought us weapons of mass destruction. And in this connection, I will say that unbridled AI might also prove to be very destructive for mankind. But that is a topic for another discussion. Suffice it for now to say that history tells us that humans are untrustworthy, to put it mildly. And if the human brain concocts the AI machine or the human-like droid, what is to stop the evil nature in man from finding its way into the inner-workings of a mass of circuitry encased in the carbon-fiber housing of the droid skull?

In any case, let's look at this Bell Curve that indicates that 99.97% of all "data" is contained within 3 standard deviations of the mean. This applies to measurable distribution of human intelligence as well.[21]

---

[21] See, https://en.wikipedia.org/wiki/Normal_distribution

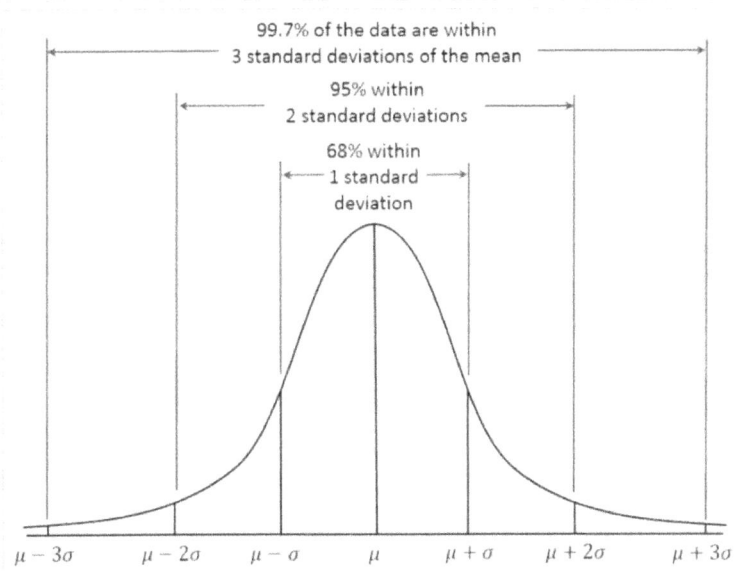

What I am saying is that the broad arc of human achievement is a product of solo and collaborative brain power; that is all attributable to a small number of individuals whose IQ was between µ + 2σ and µ + 3σ.

This level of human intelligence has been responsible the following kinds of achievements of consequence, for good and for ill, before the "digital" revolution.

Pre-Industrial Revolution
- Abaci
- Hindu-Arabic numeral system
- Algebra and geometry
- Building major cities
- Creating centers of commerce
- Channeling water / harnessing water power
- Celestial navigation
- Metallurgy
- Financial systems

- Armaments
- Agriculture
- Steam power

Industrial Revolution (c. 1760 – 1860)
- Logarithm Slide Rule
- Chemical manufacturing
- Iron production
- Textile weaving looms
- Machine tools
- Steam-powered ships, locomotives, machinery, factories
- Electric motor
- Incandescent light
- Internal combustion engine

Second Industrial Revolution (aka Technological Revolution, c. 1870 - 1914)
- Bessemer process for producing steel
- Manufacture of interchangeable parts
- Telegraph
- High-way systems
- Automobile
- Manned Flight
- Sewage, water, gas systems
- Electrical power
- Telephone
- Factory production and assembly line
- Electrification of manufacturing

Digital Revolution, c. 1947 to present day
- Transistor
- Digital Computer

- Internet
- Cell phone/tablet, smart watch, etc.

And, to be a bit more inclusive in listing our "revolutions," one must also call attention to the following—the cursory explication of each readily available in Wikipedia:[22]

- Liquid modernity
- Network society
- Human Capital society (knowledge = capital)

These advances in human accomplishment were done through trial and error, imaginative thinking, with lots of failures to be sure. But many of them, of the most impressive it can be argued, were accomplished without the assistance of a digital machine of any kind.

There is no disputing that everything since Babbage and Lovelace is also the product of high-g individual men and women working alone and in collaboration. But it has been demonstrated for hundreds of years that office workers of above-average intelligence trained to use low-tech office machines can run the Enterprise as well as those accessing ERP apps and data via the Cloud.

Let us take a closer look at the tried, proven, older, simpler way that men and women used to run the business.

---

[22] See, https://en.wikipedia.org/wiki/Post-industrial_society; see also, https://en.wikipedia.org/wiki/The_Information_Age:_Economy,_Society_and_Culture

The old, the simple, the tried-and-proven visual analog processes

The point in the above gloss of specific major human advancements is this: the human brain made each "revolution" possible. Consider the well-known achievements of early mass-production of the automobile. I have in mind in particular the fact that the human intellect alone produced the basic planning behind Henry Ford's assembly line turning out Model Ts and As. And Ford and Company did so long before MRP I and II arrived in the 1990s, and before SAP and Baan offered manufacturing "mixed model sequencing," "supply chain management," "production planning," not to mention the inventory advantages of in such concepts from Japan as Kanban, Kaizen, and the many offshoots under the rubric of "Lean Manufacturing".[23]

---

[23] Ford's moving assembly line is the breakthrough concept that lies behind all modern assembly practices. See YouTube for excellent footage, this being one of many: https://www.youtube.com/watch?v=yK1j487IED0

Ford Plant, 1923, Magneto Assembly Line: Kanban and Lean Concepts of Yesteryear[24]

During World War II, airplane manufacturing occurred on a vast scale and would not have been possible without planning the complex process of bringing material and workers together and managing the war machinery enterprise to produce Boeing's B-29—the Super Fortress, arguably the most complex machine produced during the Second World War.

---

[24] See: https://en.wikipedia.org/wiki/Assembly_line#Simple_example

"Exploded" B-29 off Wichita production line showing the main sub-assemblies.[25]

World War Two saw the rapid development and use of digital and electronic computers, which led to computing systems and machine instruction punch cards and eventually software.[26] The Genie was out of the bottle in no time, and the rest is, well, just a matter of signing up for the Cloud, the SaaS provisioning, the one's very own Data Schema floating in logical isolation in the even vast Data Lake.

However, behind all this wonderous achievement is the same driving force: the human brain.

So, let's become Imagineers and take a hard look at what the human computer can imagine as a radically different way to run the enterprise.

---

[25] See, https://en.wikipedia.org/wiki/Battle_of_Kansas

[26] See for overview of analog and advent of digital computers, ENIAC and MANIAC, used at the Manhattan Project:
https://www.atomicheritage.org/history/computing-and-manhattan-project

Yesterday's paper forms and today's digital forms contain the same information

Open any current business software application module and you will see a "form." They have the "look and feel" of Windows GUI, which means these forms are very modern, very friendly looking, something you might not mind looking at daily if you are a purchasing clerk, an AP worker-bee, an accountant, whatever.

The form below is from *perfect forms*, one of many companies in the business of selling business forms that can be tailored to meet the customer's needs and then automated and run on the office computer.

In this example, the simple form is used to create and process a PO.[27]

---

[27] There are internet companies offering "forms" that can be purchased and used to run the business. The form shown if from Perfect Forms, and their product offerings can be viewed at: http://try.perfectforms.com/form-building-software/

![Purchase Order form screenshot showing fields: Requested By (Applicant: Devin Roach, Applicant E-mail: droach@perfectforms.com, Manager, Manager E-mail, Department, Required Date, Reference) and Order Details table (Description, Quantity, Price, Value) with Total: 0.00]

Here is a more complex form taken from Infor's LN ERP product[28], this one for creating a sales order:

---

[28] See training presentation on LN functionality on YouTube: https://www.youtube.com/watch?v=ros6m2BBI84

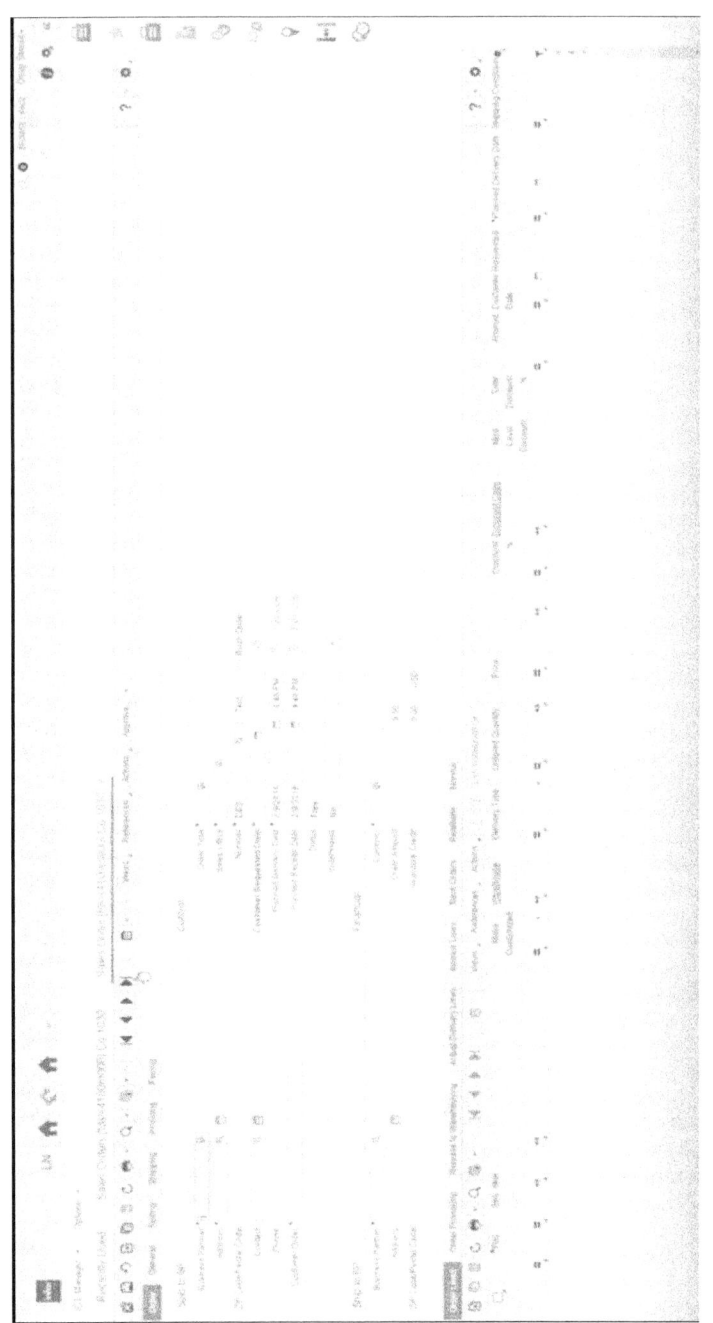

Major ERP packages from the likes of SAP, Oracle, and Infor contain thousands of such forms in application suites that encompass the data entry required to operate the business in HR, AP, Supply Chain, Finance, Pay Roll, Research, and so forth.[29]

Here is one from SAP used to create a work center.[30]

---

[29] See also Open Source ERP providers who offer their clients similar functional software to run the back office at a much less cost than what the major vendors of ERP packaged software charge for use licensing, implementation and upgrade consulting fees, maintenance cost, and much more. See: http://www.enterpriseappstoday.com/erp/slideshows/ten-open-source-erp-options.html

[30] See, https://www.tutorialspoint.com/sap_pp/sap_pp_tutorial.pdf

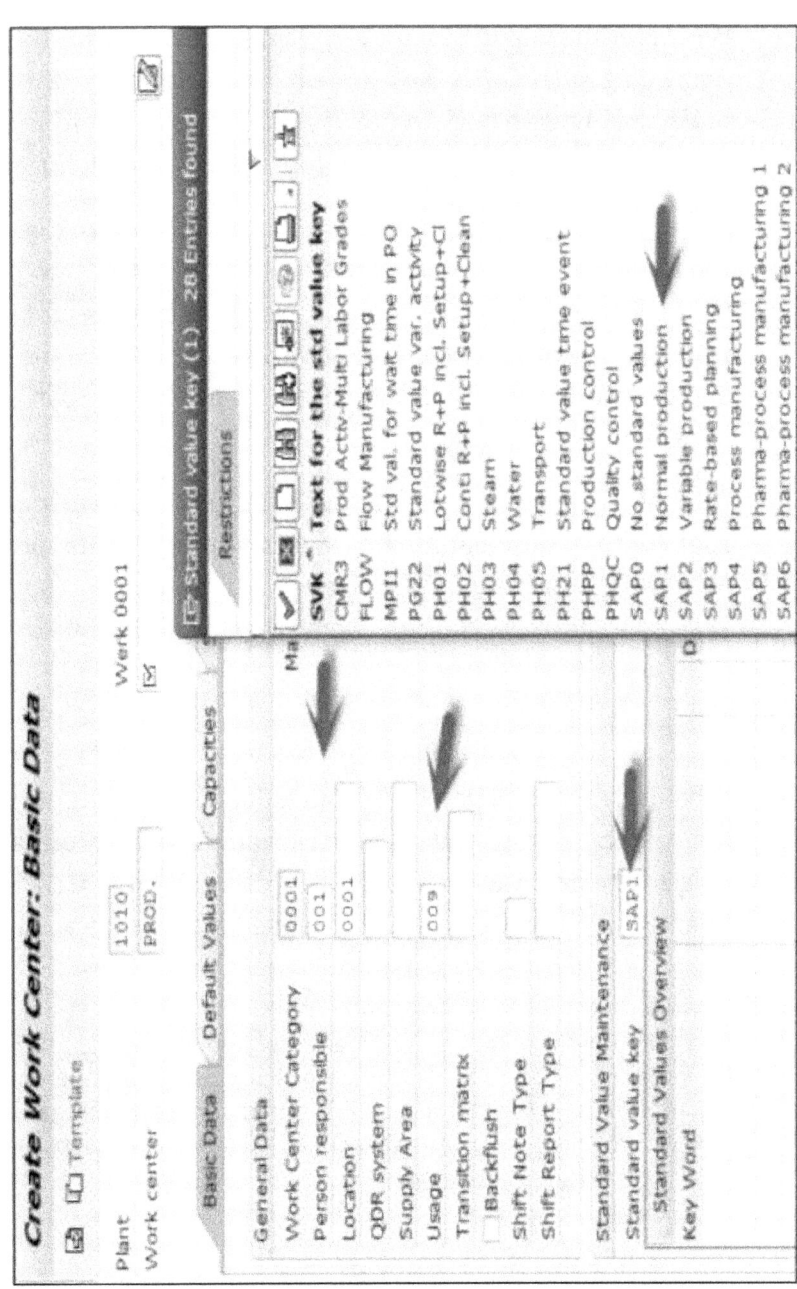

Whatever the vendor, whatever the number of forms, however many data entry fields they contain, how colorful the GUI or how much they harken back to the days of Green Screen forms, they all are electronic versions of their forbearers: PAPER forms.

And in many cases, it is possible to trace the electronic version to the layout functionality of its predecessor business form printed by the local shop and delivered to the office manager for safe keeping. But once the bright idea was born to digitize the form and put the image on the computer screen, the life span of the paper version was doomed.

After all, the mantra was and continues to be "go paperless my soul, for that is the path to heavenly salvation." Or its corollary: "businesses that rely on paper today will rely on bankruptcy lawyers tomorrow—which is worse than being in Hell."[31]

Is data on paper relational—to the human brain?

What is a relational database[32]? Relational databases use the idea of tables (rows and columns) in with to store information. This arrangement was the brainchild of an IBM research scientist, E. F. Codd. In 1970, he devised the schema and it has

---

[31] See story on NH physician losing license because she does not use a computer in her home-based practice. This illustrates the absurdity of mandating a set level of technology in the practice of healing arts and sciences. Hopefully her license will be re-instated by the NH courts.
http://www.fox5ny.com/news/doctor-who-refuses-to-use-computers-loses-medical-license

[32] For an explanation that is easy to understand, see:
https://computer.howstuffworks.com/question599.htm

replaced the previous structure, which was a flat text file of data elements separated by tabs, commas, colons, or pipes.

The chief advantage of Codd's notion is that data in tables is easy to query using certain logic commands, commonly called Sequential Query Language, of SQL. The output is what everyone seemingly cannot get enough of: the data-laden report.

Basically, it is the queried data in a formatted structure of columns and rows. Here are examples of the old linear text database and the relational database, or the Relational Database Management System (RDMS) that is used to mine and report on data once it has been hand-keyed by "back office workers" into one of today's ERP systems.

And here is a sample Text File report[33]

```
Sepal length   Sepal width    Petal length    Petal width    Species
5.1     3.5    1.4     0.2    I. setosa
4.9     3.0    1.4     0.2    I. setosa
4.7     3.2    1.3     0.2    I. setosa
4.6     3.1    1.5     0.2    I. setosa
5.0     3.6    1.4     0.2    I. setosa
```

The TSV plain text above corresponds to the following tabular data:

Sepal length	Sepal width	Petal length	Petal width	Species
5.1	3.5	1.4	0.2	I. setosa
4.9	3.0	1.4	0.2	I. setosa
4.7	3.2	1.3	0.2	I. setosa
4.6	3.1	1.5	0.2	I. setosa
5.0	3.6	1.4	0.2	I. setosa

---

[33] For discussion of delimiters, see: https://en.wikipedia.org/wiki/Tab-separated_values

Here is the schema that evolved out of Codd's paper:

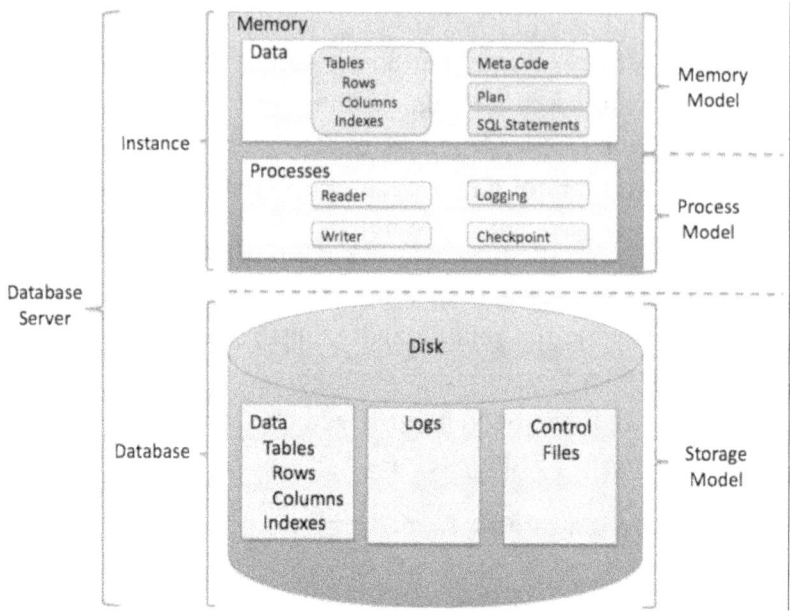

And a computer-screen image of an SQL RDMS report[34]

---

[34] Sample SQL report image from: https://en.wikipedia.org/wiki/Database

And here is one of the most sophisticated and widely used file and retrieval systems: the numerical taxonomy and ease of use of the Dewey Decimal System[35]

Dewey Decimal Classification to Library of Congress Classification
(General Outline)

Dewey	LC	General Subject	Dewey	LC	General Subject
000, 040, 080	AC	General Collections	570	GN, QH	Anthropology, Nat. Hist
010, 020, 090	Z	Library Science			
030	AE	Encyclopedias	580	QK	Botany
050	AP	Periodicals	590	QL	Zoology
060	AS	Academies, Societies	600	T-TX	Technology
070	PN	Literature (Gen.)	610	R	Medicine (General)
100	B-BJ	Philosophy (Gen.)	620	TA	Engineering
110-120	BD	Speculative Philosophy	630	S, HD	Agriculture, Land Use
130, 150	BF	Psychology	640	TX	Home Economics
140, 180, 190	B	Philosophy (Gen.)	650	HF	Commerce
160	BC	Logic	660	TP	Chemical Technology
170	BJ	Ethics	670, 680	TS, HD	Manufactures
200, 210, 290	BL	Religions, Mythology	690	TH	Building Construction
220	BS	The Bible	700	N	Visual arts
230	BT	Doctrinal Theology	710	SB	Plant culture
240, 250	BV	Practical Theology	720	NA	Architecture
260, 270	BR	Christianity	730	NB	Sculpture
280	BX	Christian Denominations	740	NC	Drawing, Design
300	H	Soc. Sci. (General)	750	ND	Painting
310	HA	Statistics	760	NE	Print Media
320	J	Gen. Legislative papers	770	TR	Photography
330	HB	Economic Theory	780	M	Music
340	K	Law	790	GV	Recreation, Leisure
350	JF-JS	Political Institutions	800	PN	Literature (General)
360	HN, HV	Social History, Soc. Pathology	810	PS	American Literature
			820	PR	English Literature
370	L	Education (General)	830	PT	German Literature
380	HD	Industries, Land Use, Labor	840, 850, 860	PQ	French, Italian, Spanish and Portuguese Literature
390	GT	Manners and customs			
400, 410	P	Philology, Linguistics	870, 880	PA	Ancient Literatures
420	PE	English Language	890	PK-PL	Other Literatures
430	PF	Germanic Languages	900, 930	D	History (General)
440, 450, 460	PC	Romanic Languages	910	G-GF	Geography
470, 480	PA	Classical Philology	920	CT	Biography
490	PK	Indo-Iranian Lang. and Lit.	940	D, DA-DR	History of Europe
500	Q	Science (General)			
510	QA	Mathematics	950	DS	History of Asia
520	QB	Astronomy	960	DT	History of Africa
530	QC	Physics	970	E, F	History of Americas
540	QD	Chemistry	980	F	History of U.S.
550, 560	QE	Geology	990	DS, DU	History of Oceania

---

[35] See: https://en.wikipedia.org/wiki/Dewey_Decimal_Classification

What Henry Ford can (and should) teach today's CEO

Now consider the report below (created by the author when he had nothing better to do) that presents on hand inventory, WIP, and demand forecast for the required number of hickory wheel spokes to meet the projected 1923 production runs for all Model T offerings made in the assembly plants in the River Rouge complex in Dearborn, MI.

River Rouge

January 2, 1923
Wheel Spoke Inventory Planning for Production

Model T (all models) total sold, 1922 (based on Calendar year):	1,301,067
Average sales per month, 1922, all models combined:	108,422
Mr. Ford anticipates a 25% increase of model sales in 1923 = 1,301,067 / 25%:	325,267
Mr. Ford anticipates a total production run, all models:	1,626,334
Mr. Ford anticipates average sales per month, 1923, all models combined:	135,528
Mr. Ford plans total sales on average per month (average $375 per model):	$50,823,200
Mr. Ford plans total sales, all models combined, 1923 (average $375 per model):	$609,875,250

----

12 spokes per wheel: 48 hickory spokes
Spoke shop foreman, Mr. Amos Asher, plans to allow per model for damaged spokes: 60 hickory spokes
(Mr. Ford has approved Mr. Asher's safety margin, based on detailed records kept by Mr. Asher over the past ten years as spoke shop foreman)

Counted spokes on hand, finished and ready for the line -- Use in January	8,131,680
Counted spokes on hand (need sanding and oiling) -- Use in February, March	16,263,360
Counted split and R.S. billets on hand -- Use in April	8,131,680
Counted green billets on hand -- Use May, June	16,263,360

Orders placed by Mr. A. Asher for Shag Bark hickory billets – # ordered
Order Date / Hickory Source by State

1/3/1923	/ Michigan	July, August	16,263,360
1/4/1923	/ Ohio	September, October	16,263,360
1/5/1923	/ Kentucky	November, December	16,263,360
1/6/1923	/ Tennessee	January 1924	8,131,680

Mr. Ford approved on January 2, 1923 order for green hickory billets: 56,921,760
Total number of unfinished spokes on hand and green billets ordered for
wheel assembly requirements February 1923 – January 1924: 97,580,160

Mr. Ford approved on January 2, 1923 order for green billet spokes cost
at $0.001 cents each to meet order needs : July 1923 – January 1924: $56,921.00
Mr. Ford approved Mr. Asher's cost of $0.001 cents each to finish all fabrication
for wheel spokes to meet order needs: February 1923 through January 1924: $97,580.00

Mr. Ford approved total cost for green billet order and all spoke fabrication cost
through January 1924: $154,501.00
----

cc: Mr. Ford
　　Mr. Asher, Spoke Fabrication Foreman
　　Mr. Smithers, Bookkeeping
　　Miss Daniels, File Clerk

ktk: HF January 2, 1923

Wheel spoke inventory and production planning: an informative vignette

My fictitious supply chain management "analytical report" from Henry Ford's era has all the essential features and benefits for the user that SQL reports generated out of the RDMS concept possess. Which begs the question: how was it possible to produce such a report before computers, before relational databases, before sophisticated inventory management software existed?

The CEO enters the conference room where his key executive team is assembled. The CEO hands out the "Wheel Spoke Inventory Planning for Production" report. He gives them a few minutes to look it over and then he asks them a series of questions along these lines.

Then the CEO begins the "conversation."

The question I pose to you is this: how were accurate physical inventory counts possible in 1922/23? Consider that the number of hickory wheel spokes, at 12 per wheel, four wheels per car, ran into the millions required monthly. Talk about Kanban, Kaizen, just in time inventory schemas versus Ford's proven perpetual inventory model, clearly evident in the above inventory planning document, based on anticipated sales and spoke needs, again all based on historical records. And then there is the matter of the cost, security, and reliability of "accurate human" data then vs. "accurate machine" machine today!

Bringing the Dearborn assembly line to a standstill for a week or two because of a shortage of hickory wheel spokes would have been the talk of Dearborn, and the press of the day would have preserved this shocking news, and we would know about it even today, via Google, of course! Same thing applies to us today. Wall Street is always looking for a whiff of downside, of executive mismanagement of capital and human resources.

So how was this level of production planning and material forecasting possible without today's data storage? Without analytical reports coming out of data cubes? Without software algorithms that recommend purchase time-gates to ensure adequate lead time needed to have on hand what is needed?

If this was all possible for the very successful Ford enterprise back in the 1920s, what does that tell us about the cost we expend today for the same basic information, whether in manufacturing, healthcare, or finance? And before you answer, consider this: is it feasible and valid to take the complexity of any situation and then simplify it by breaking it down into its basic components? Is this what happens when Big Data is parsed and rendered into a "report" that the business decision-maker can understand, trust, and then use as the basis to make an informed decision that comes out of that data?

Well, I ask you: is there another way to get done what we must do, and do with excellence and quality across the board, and yet not have to rely on big data, complex integrated and expensive ERP systems? Should we think about what we really need and all the various ways we can get there? After all, you are asking me to approve over the next five years a SaaS Cloud contract that will cost millions of precious dollars of capital outlay? And then what happens beyond the initial five years? An upgrade? A different kind of Cloud? What is the cost-benefit trade-off? Has anyone done that study and produced reliable numbers to base our decision on?

One can imagine the startled looks on the faces of the CIO, CTO, CDO, COO, Director Supply Chain Management, et al. in the little mis en scene. I leave it to your imagination to conjure the range of explanations they would offer as to how Ford could do it without any reliance on any kind of computer other than the human brain. And any kind of database and data retrieval or reports based on them other than the handwritten tabulations in the file system under the management of Ms. Daniels, Ford Motor Company file clerk.

The way IT could be?

What are the options when enveloped in the hyped-fog of expensive ERP, big data, and the cloudscape?

To me, the obvious answer is that there are several options worthy of your serious consideration.

All major ERP systems offer core applications that span Finance, Supply Chain, Human Resources, and Pay Roll. All businesses today need one or more of these application suites. Most need all of them. But Ford used his version of these ERP applications without the cost and security risks posed to having systems in the Cloud, or behind the firewall on-premise where the hackers or the disgruntled employee in IT can expose it all to the light of the world, or mine and sell, or just destroy for the crazy fun of it or out of misguided (and illegal) vengefulness.

Let's look at the options that the CIO/CFO/CEO/CDO will never give a thought to because of their buying into the standard notion that only Big ERP will make it possible to run the business.

Jim, MIT, the IPC, and ATAP

But first, let's spend a few minutes visiting the faintest beginnings of a morality play, of what Shakespeare called the "playing cards dealt kings and knaves alike," and what Freud called "the willful suspension of subconscious ego constraints."

Here is the imaginary realm I present to you for your amusement and, perchance, your very own private "thought stimulation."

Now let us return from that brief excursion into the theatre of the IPC/ATAP and look briefly at the "current IT zeitgeist." As we conduct the following analysis, I suggest a point-counter-point frame of mind, keeping Jim alive in your mind on the one hand, and what follows on the other.

It is early Monday morning and the UPS truck pulls up to the IPC (integration processing center) right on time. Jim, a recent MIT graduate and an IPC intern, checks the purchase order against the shipping order and seeing that all is correct, signs for the usual supplies: boxes of yellow and white legal pads, student notebooks, pens, pencils, erasable white board markers, boxes of white and yellow chalk, meeting planners, and desk top calendars.

He pushes the cart into the IPC store room and puts the office supplies away. He is just about done when Mary, the Senior Resource Coordinator, comes in and helps herself to a stack of legal pads and white board red and blue erasable markers. "Oh, Jim, stop by my desk when you are done in here. I want to spend a few minutes with you, get your thinking on how things are going for you, now that you have been here six months, okay?"

Jim, still feeling lucky to be a new hire in the coolest IPC in the Valley, stops at Mary's desk as asked. Sitting in the chair beside her desk, he watched as she put the Mont Blanc Rouge et Noir down on the legal pad. He looked at the red pen and wondered if only SRCs rated such a writing instrument.

"Jim, I want you to tell me how you honestly feel about the concept of IPC." She made a circular motion in the air, signifying the space and time around them made up of the IPC. Jim quickly looked around the large open space, at the executives sitting at

their desks, at the clustered key team members in Human Resources, Supply Chain Management, Finance sitting at theirs, and, in the center of the room about the size of a basketball court, he saw the ATAP (Applied Thought Application Processing) group, the team he would join when his cross-functional internship ended.

"What I mean is, I want you to tell me your thoughts about IPC, what you like about it, and I want your candid thoughts about what you don't like as well."

"Well, to be honest, I had my doubts at first." Mary smiles, nods encouragingly. "Yes, of course, and?" Jim goes on, deciding to tell her exactly how he feels about the concepts behind the IPC. "I mean, it was an adjustment for me, as it would be for anyone, coming to work here, in the IPC. Seeing the signage on the glass front entrance doors, "Warning: IPC is a Silicon Chip Free Environment: No Laptops, Cell Phones, or Cloud-linked Devices Permitted." At first, the picture of the lap top in a cloud shape with a diagonal line through it, like you see for guns and smoking, well, to be honest, that notice was a real shocker every morning I walked in the door. Even though I knew about IPC before I interviewed, the decals on the door were a daily reminder to me of just how different it was from other places."

Mary leaned forward and smiled again. "And now, after six months at IPC?"

"Well, to be honest, Mary, at first I felt I had been deprived of a Constitutional right, having to leave my cell at home or in the car. And it was strange at first having no desktops or laptops at work, no printers, and of course no email. And not even a pretense of an IT department at all. Thinking back on my transition to what

my former colleagues would call the 'dark ages', it was all hard to adjust to at first. And on top of all that, I missed my daily dashboard analytics."

Jim fell silent and then Mary asked, her tone now serious: "So to sum it all up, Jim, what is your assessment of IPC now, of your internship work? What do you look forward to at IPC?"

Determined to tell her the unvarnished truth, Jim looked her in the eye and said: "Where I worked before coming to IPC, which was at DataLytics in Boston, that whole concept was 180 degrees out of phase with IPC. Looking back on DL, and comparing it to my time here at IPC, and what I get to do here compared to what I did there, there is no comparison. Here, I am expected to use my brain, to think, to create, to propose ideas on how to best restructure the Enterprise. Back there, I was just another MIT grad who spent his time turning paper processes into Cloud based apps linked to seas of data and worrying about security from hackers and all the while meeting the hype of marketing. Here, in the IPC, people like me spend their time creating with pen and paper the heuristics to help people make decisions completely outside of high-tech, without software that inhibits self-reliance, retards the ability to think for oneself. At IPC, it does not get much different than that. So that's my view, Mary."

Mary grinned and asked, "And what about AI, where are you on AI now, Jim? I ask because I remember, when ATAP and I interviewed you, you had a very positive view of the promise of AI."

Jim smiled at Mary, and like she had done when he first took his seat at her desk, he repeated her gesture, moving his hand in a circle, and said: "This is where it's at, Mary. This is real intelligence. This is natural intelligence. This is human intelligence. This is man over machine."

Mary pushed back from her desk and stood up. Jim did the same. She extended her hand and, as they shook hands, she said, "Today is your last day as an intern. I want you to report to Joan, Ahmed, and Frank. They are anxious for you to join them in ATAP."

Jim liked what he was hearing. "This is great news, thanks."

Mary concluded their chat by giving him specific good news: "You will start there as a Level 1 Research Associate. Your white board sessions will begin tomorrow in the Henry Ford room. I wish you all the best as a member of the Applied Thought team."

Jim smiled, knowing he was on his way, at last, to ATAP.

In the Model T Room

When Jim entered the Model T room at eight the next morning, Ahmed asked him what he made of what was on the white board. Jim looked and the only thing that came to mind was a tepee on fire. "Exactly, it could well be a tepee on fire," Frank said to Ahmed. "Not that, no, look more closely." Neither Jim nor Frank offered another guess. Ahmed frowned at Frank and then wrote above the squiggle of intersecting red lines with flecks of black marker: "B_ _n_ _ _ _ a _." Ahmed said, "that's your clue. You finish it." He handed the marker to Jim. Then Joan entered the room, looked at the board, and said, "Ahmed, did you go this year? When he nodded "yes," she replied, "You should have told me, we could have left nothing behind together. . . including our sanity."

Jim handed the marker back to Ahmed and took a seat while Ahmed erased the board and then wrote:

"Burning Man is a Function of the TWO SD Rule of Thumb Without God in the Mix"

Ahmed then wrote on the board "Darwin, cellular differentiation, and the role of environment."

Ahmed asked Jim what he thought, and Jim offered that if man's nature was "fixed and a constant, that meant that despite evolutionary progress. . ." at which point Frank interrupted Jim and added that "only man was capable of love and the good it brought about in the world, but. . ." and he in turn was interrupted by Joan, who said "there is no way around the fact that history shows that no matter the SD to the right or to the left of the median, that men and women are hard wired to be destructive, which is why we have still, even here at IPC, we have an HR department." And Frank added, "Our very own savior, Mother Mary the People Coordinator."

When the laughter ended, Ahmed wrote on the board, "And it was foreordained that Mary, Savior of ATAP, would send us James of MIT."

Ahmed then handed Jim a printed list of topics that they would cover in the four weeks set up to bring him into the working ATAP group. The topics for weeks 1-4 were:

Discussion Topics and Reading Assignments

Week 1:

- *Today -- Monday: What is the history and purpose of IPC/ATAP? What are the challenges facing IPC and ATAP? What are the near- and long-term business opportunities?*
- *Tuesday: Read and be prepared to discuss: Isaac Asimov's "How do People get New Ideas," MIT Technology Review (it is in the IPC library)*
- *Wednesday: Artificial and Human Intelligence as Tools for Work and Creativity in the World of Work: Promises, Limits, Boundaries, Outcomes, Real vs. Imaginary Dangers and Risks*
- *Thursday: Defining what is "meaningful work" in the context of today's digital corporate world? What are the implications of social media driving the ever-increasing human-machine bondage?*
- *Friday: Open exchange of ideas covering above topics*

Week 2:

- *Monday: What barriers must be overcome if IPC/ATAP's "thought product" is to gain an audience in Corporate America?*
- *Tuesday: Data—what is it? What does/can data mean to machines? To us?*
- *Wednesday: Data decisions—what are the chief fallacies of decision-making that is based on small- and big-data?" What the vendors offer us today: who understands data, who uses data, who wins and who fails by data reliance*
- *Thursday: Data modeling and AI learning machines—How can humans program AI data learning "machines" if we ourselves cannot ascertain "data meaning" out of millions*

of data elements? Is it the blind leading the blind? How can predictive algorithms/data models based on any amount of data rely on statistical outcome predictions if the very data feeding the model is generated in a wholly random manner? Is conditioned by a myriad of factors, some of which can be known, some of which cannot? How to clear and validate data in whole or in part first? What are the practical threshold limits of extrapolation in the workplace? In the Stock Market? In futures trading? In any domain?

- *What are the inherent limits of Data Science?*
- *Who can understand the output of the entire data mining/modeling process? Who can make decisions based on the outcome? Where does "trust" enter into the picture, between business executives and "data scientists" presenting their "findings?"*
- *Friday: Open exchange of ideas on any topic from weeks 1 and 2*

Week 3:

- *Monday: The workplace: what it used to be, what it is now, what it looks like it will become*
- *Tuesday: What is the value/ethics of using standardized IQ testing as a required step in the recruitment/hiring process? What will ever-increasing reliance on robotics, computers, data, and technology at work mean for the average and less-than-average workers when measured for IQ? How will the future of work be changed by technology? Will there always be a job slot for them?*
- *Wednesday: How many people are REALLY needed to run the back office in any corporation of any size and physical*

distribution? Finance, HR, Supplies, Legal, Operations, Planning, Payroll, etc.? How to review and establish their minimum qualifications, education, level of intelligence, experience?
- *Thursday: What are the core attributes needed to be an executive, and how many executives in which roles are Necessary to lead the corporation of any size? Finance, manufacturing, academe, etc.*
- *Friday: Jim leads discussion of topics of interest to him covered in Weeks 1-3*

Week 4:

- *Monday: Can off the shelf (OTS) "low tech" systems and tools be used to run the Enterprise in today's machine and data based corporate world? What are the tradeoffs in terms of efficiency, security, and productivity?*
- *Tuesday: What are the short and long-term cost trade-offs of low versus high-tech to the Enterprise? What is the user-accessibility threshold for the workforce that is representative of the spread of intelligence as portrayed by the standard psychometric Bell Curve? What are the implications of "dumbing down" the systems, the data, the interface between human and machine?*
- *Wednesday: What are the barriers facing IPC to get Corporate America to listen to the ATAP approach? How can the barriers be removed? What are the benefits and the liabilities to Corporate America if it adopts in whole or in part one of the ATAP business/technology models?*
- *Thursday: Authoring white papers and Thought Articles at ATAP: General Guidelines*

- *Friday: Jim presents to the ATAP team his assessment of what ATAP means to him, to PIC, and to the world of work in Corporate America today and in the future. He also presents his reasons for wanting to remain at IPC/ATAP, or his reasons for wanting to leave and return to any number of positions available to him as a graduate of MIT with DataLytics on his resume.*

The IPC/ATAP vignette—what does it signify? What is its value?

First, there is a very low probability that the "low-to-no-tech" based IPC (Integration Processing Center) depicted in the brief tableau presented just now exists today. The same can be said about the ATAP (Applied Thought Application Processing) group that Jim is on the verge of joining.

This claim, that IPCs and ATAPs as shown in the vignette are rare indeed in today's corporate world, rests on the basic fact that **the IPC/ATAP's primary purpose is to eschew the Cloud, Big Data, AI and all such kindred notions and technologies** for the **low-to-no-tech-based-process** of sharing with one another the best that comes out of their individual and group reading, writing, thinking, idea creation, and peer critiquing.

To put it another way, their *raison d'être*, their reason for existing, is to come up with simple ways to run the business with as little to do with digitized electronics, data, cloud-schemas, hacking, data loss, anti-breach layering schemas, loss recovery mechanisms, and so forth. They understand this technology, have worked in and with it, of course, but they choose to counter-balance its need in their pursuit of viable alternatives to its pervasive use, high-cost, security risks, and built-in obsolescence for hardware, software, and data storage/retrieval systems in any way linked to the Web.

Their library has in it all leading technology journals, from the high-brow ("Epistemology and Data Mining") right down to *CIO*.

Even radical alternatives, of course, and especially in the insistence that the members of IPC/ATAP leave the modern world of "electronic life" at home when they travel to the office daily. Instead of internal email at work, they talk face to face; and instead of cell phones at the ready, they are banned from the building, as are all other electronic devices.

The closest one comes to a group of people within today's corporate world—not think tanks, not R&D firms—is the "Center of Excellence" (CoE), a phrase designed to conjure visions of savvy members of the organization's leadership who meet regularly to further the vision and define the process improvements needed to achieve corporate objectives in a highly-efficient, cost effective manner.

The CoE is typically made up of some or all of the following:

- business analysts
- software engineers
- operations leaders and SMEs from finance, HR, purchasing, et al.
- IT leadership
- PMO leadership (project focused)
- EPMO leadership (Enterprise focused)
- COO, CIO, CFO, CDO, CTO (business strategy focused)

The major difference between Jim's IPC/ATAP and the typical CoE is obvious. The CoE is grounded in and more than not fully-supportive of all-things high-tech, held to be the essential life-blood of the Body Enterprise.

The ATAP, on the other hand, does not seek to foster technology as the basis upon which the business operates. Rather, it explores ways to accomplish what the CoE seeks to accomplish, but with as little (to none) of the current standard bill of fare menu recommending, and often mandating, a six course meal of Big Data, Cloud Computing, AI, Machine Learning, SOC1 and SOC2 security, and the usual ingestion of as many of the other hyped tidbit concepts as possible.

Let's explore in brief the mix of "high-tech" that has become indispensable in today's corporate America, and indeed across all developed countries participating in the Global economy that is in many ways one of the major elements in what has been termed the *New World Order*.

The paper option = the human (brainiac?) option

Let's look at using paper for HR functions—not for electronic healthcare records--in a Health Care not-for-profit that employees 5,000 people. Also, let's consider the same approach for a US manufacturing company that employees 1500 people, half in the US, half in Canada.

The first thing needed in either instance (healthcare or manufacturing) is to create a personnel file sheet on each employee. That basic information is as follows:

- Legal name(s)
- Nationality
- Work status/permits
- US SS number, or equivalent non-US number for tax withholding purposes
- Marital status
- Number and ages of legal dependents and relationship to employee
- Address of current residence
- Contact information (phone numbers)
- Current health insurance provider, if any, and policy number(s)
- Banking information for purposes of automatic pay deposit
- Emergency contact, relationship, and contact information
- Educational attainments (degrees, certificates)
- Physical work handicaps, if any
- Criminal record, if any

What it takes to make this option viable is *quality all around*, which is likely why it will never return to the world of business large and small, except for the rare outfit whose management eschews the computer age for who knows what reason, valid or otherwise. *Quality all around* means what, exactly?

Here are a few areas in which it is imperative for the paper system to work reasonably well in today's world:

- Intelligent
- Organized
- Exacting
- Mindful

- Focused
- Decisive
- Knowledgeable
- Honest
- Industrious
- Thoughtful
- Empowered
- Empowering
- Creative
- Educated
- Trained
- Skilled
- Dynamic
- Self-directed
- Self-motivated
- Self-disciplined

And how many of these wonderous specimens will the enterprise need?

Here is my own table of human resource requirements. It shows the required number of employees who possess the right degree of genetically-derived IQ and socialized behavioral attributes that combine to comprise the traits that were needed to lift early *homo sapiens* from the dark cave in western Europe into the light and warmth of a modest home in Anywhere America.

# Employees in the enterprise	Accounting (aka Finance)	Stores (Supply Chain)	Personnel (Human Capital Management)	Payroll	Middle and Upper Management	Senior Executives
10-99	1	1	1	1	3	1
100-499	2	2	2	2	3	2
500-9,999	3	3	3	3	3	2
10,000 – 49,999	4	4	3	3	3	3
50,000 – 99,999	5	5	5	5	5	4

There is no earthly reason (or extra-terrestrial, for that matter) that a properly structured set of business processes carried out by employees possessing the above traits and abilities who use basic spreadsheets on basic laptops or dumb work screens cannot handle the job at a fraction of today's bloated staffing models in academe and across corporate America.

Let's dive into that arcane world of the human capital resources worker and look at what headcount there might well be (not all what it is today).

Consider a corporation with 10,000 employees. How many FTEs are hired daily? What is the daily FTE turnover? Obviously, the answers will vary across the spectrum by kind of non-seasonal workforce by industry vertical market (what they make and sell).

Posit that between turnover and new FTE demand the level of annual headcount change is 10 per cent. That is 1,000 employees, or on average 3.8 FTEs per day to be "processed" in or out of the workforce over the course of a five-day work week over 52 weeks. Can you imagine any situation wherein one intelligent and energetic HR staffer could not process and manage this rate of churn in the workforce? At four per day, that means 2 hours per FTE to gather key information from, process in or out (badge turn in/creation, paper work for benefits, pay roll, taxation, so forth), and pass along to their department where the leaders there will show them the ropes, provide needed training, so on.

For a workforce of 100,000, that is 38.8 employees to process a day. With an HR staff of three, that is ten each per day. That would keep them busy for sure. But how many companies experience annual churn rate of 10 percent, or 39 FTEs a day all year long that must be brought on-board and mustered out. As shown below, churn was about 8.8 percent for 2.8 million workers across the US in 2016.?[36]

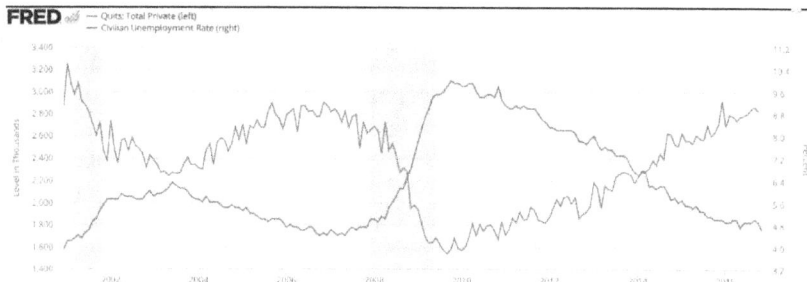

Take the typical bloated headcount and under-utilized faculty and staff in higher-education, and the high-turnover rate and constant recruitment efforts that are needed to keep the business running, the students engaged, and the alumni contributing.[37]

Consider the low churn rate at the Medical College at The Ohio State Medical College:

---

[36] See, https://en.wikipedia.org/wiki/Turnover_(employment)

[37] See, https://www.businesswire.com/news/home/20160922005406/en/Study-Case-Employee-Engagement-Higher-Education-Institutions

". . . the size of the faculty at the College of Medicine, most of whom serve as doctors at the medical center, has grown from 1,792 in 2015 to 1,951 this year. Further, the turnover rate is on a downward trend and on track to be at 8 percent this year, less than the 8.9 percent median rate experienced by medical centers of comparable size."[38]

The takeaway point of this little side-excursion into deep personnel matters is this: the rate of churn is quite low and is therefore manageable by fewer HR staff than what one typically finds in Big Corporate and Big Academe. Of course, any quality-staffed HR department will project workload requirements and will outsource if and when required to get over any unexpected demands. They will be on top of:

- What is their expansion and new hire requirements?
- How are the employees recruited and what improved processes can be implemented for greater efficiency and "success rate"?
- What is the total year-over-year individual FTE on-boarding and off-loading processing time?

Answers to these key questions are not hard to come by. And knowing them with a high degree of certitude will enable the leadership in business, academe, and the professions to opt for "low tech" tool sets as opposed to Big Bucks solutions that are available via the Cloud, the Big Data, the social apps.

Put simply: low churn, or even high churn, is manageable if two or three or five quality HR staff are on hand to manage the ebb

---

[38] See, http://www.dispatch.com/news/20170516/another-faculty-letter-critical-of-ohio-state-leadership-surfaces

and flow. And they do not need big data, deep analytics, machine learning, AI, or the Cloud-based data sea to do it all. A simple basic laptop and Excel will do it without question. The cost savings of course will be of interest to the accountant in charge of calculating the bottom line; and the investor crowd and stock owners will also appreciate greater divided yield due lower overall cost to operate the enterprise as a low-tech organization that uses human brainpower rather than rely on the prevalent alternative: Marketeers panacea of all things AI, Big Data, Cloud SaaS, PaaS, and IaaS.

Ideal employee profile: high "g" above all else[39]

Clearly, the employees who can get the job done in any enterprise need to be a cut above the average in terms of high native general intelligence, or G—at least two SD to the right would be ideal (and Mensa members might be qualified if they aspire to working in the business as opposed to being underemployed so they can read more books; these employees also need to be broadly educated, which means a solid grounding in the Arts and Sciences in the old school sense where one went to state university or the small college and came out knowing quite a lot about many subjects. And how to think, read, and write, of course, above all else.

And this goes not just for the senior leadership, those who espouse to run the enterprise and serve as its executives, but for all the employees. They all need to know what you are talking about when you ask them if they have ever heard of **The Great**

---

[39] See, https://en.wikipedia.org/wiki/G_factor_(psychometrics)

Books, and if they have, if they have read any of them, or plan to do so any time soon. And if they have not, you should expect them to say they will look them up and get back to you. And they do it and they do get back to you, within a day or two, and have something to say about them.

Occupational complexity and cognitive ability[40]

The job roles by IQ ranking shown below are meant to present general categorization of the importance of IQ in the workplace.[41] The IQ range of 110 to 115 will suffice for most of the jobs needed to make the non-ERP Cloud-based enterprise run in an efficient manner. Leadership would come from the upper tier range of IQ, from 116 to 130. It is likely that this upper tier of individuals is the source for leadership across human history. Certainly, one would expect to see these individuals at the heart of the enterprise, whether it was during the Roman, Renaissance, early industrial revolution, or what today is called the Information or Digital Revolution.

---

[40] See, https://en.wikipedia.org/wiki/Cognitive_complexity

[41] The above occupational categories by IQ range are from: http://www.iqcomparisonsite.com/Occupations.aspx

Complexity and cognitive ability

- 95-86 percentile
  - IQ 130 – 116

  - Attorney, Research Analyst
  - Editor, Advertising Manager
  - Chemist, Engineer, Executive
  - Manager, Trainee,
  - Systems Analyst, Auditor

- 85-73 percentile
  - IQ 115-110

  - Copywriter, Accountant
  - Manager/Supervisor
  - Sales Manager
  - Sales, Programmer
  - Analyst, Teacher, Adjuster
  - General Manager
  - Purchasing Agent
  - Registered Nurse
  - Sales Account Executive

- 70-60 percentile
  - IQ 108-103

  - Administrative Assistant
  - Store Manager, Bookkeeper
  - Credit Clerk, Drafter, Designer
  - Lab Tester/Tech, Assistant Manager
  - General Sales, Telephone Sales
  - Secretary, Accounting Clerk,
  - Medical Debt Collection
  - Computer Operator
  - Customer Service Rep
  - Technician, Automotive Salesman
  - Clerk, Typist

And no one places much importance on the MBA, although no one will be turned down for the job because they have the degree. Same for the AA, BA, BS, MA, MS, D. Ed., M.D., Ph.D.—all of them are welcomed marks of achievement, none of them is automatically judged to be or greater value than the rest, and none is needed. The stories about college drop-outs who went on to found global enterprises of various kinds are well-known.[42]

---

[42] See: http://www.rediff.com/business/slide-show/slide-show-1-college-dropouts-who-built-business-empires/20120823.htm

Annual cost for the back-office digital-free paper enterprise

To run the business on the old, tried-and-proven paper system, here is one estimate of the cost of setting up the office equipment. (Remember, back in the day, **all companies, great and small in all areas of "work and production" around the world,** ran on the paper-centric business operating system.)

Scoffers with respect to the office that runs 'the old-fashioned way" that is presented above, admittedly in an over-simplified manner for purposes of illustrating the argument's basic tenets, should remember: Henry Ford did it. Sears, Roebuck & Co. did it. Early banks did it; early stock markets in NYC and Chicago also did it. Thousands of "enterprises did it before the computer, before ERP systems, and the databases connected to them.

Paper office filing system where data was and still is stored[43]

---

[43] See: https://en.wikipedia.org/wiki/Filing_cabinet

The low-tech option: the tinker toy ethernet / wireless intranet

Moving one step away (but not necessarily up) from the basic pen-and-paper-based operation means considering a return to the low-tech LAN system of laptops, printers, work stations, and fax machines. What would this cost, you ask? See Lisa Phifer's analysis[44] for comparative costs for ethernet and wireless LAN setup. The table below summarizes the costs.

	Ethernet	WLAN
Ethernet/PoE Port	$35	$35
Installation	$200	$250
AP	-	$1,300 (50 users)
Controller	-	$15,000 (50 APs)
Installed Cost for 100 users	$23,500	$16,585
Installed Cost for 1,000 users	$235,000	$46,700

Consider a fire in the office that consumes all the paper in the filing cabinets (which foolishly are not fire-rated, and the files had not copied weekly and stored in the CEO's locked attic in a fire-proof vault; nor was there a backup duplicate process of

---

[44] https://searchnetworking.techtarget.com/tip/Wireless-or-Ethernet-LAN-An-apples-to-apples-cost-comparison

copying and storing the files in the vault in the largest bank in town, or in a fire-rated room in a storage facility. Fire is the threat. Following that is malicious destruction of files by a current or former employee, or by an intruder hired by a competitor, a Watergate burglary motivated not by the desire for political but for commercial advantage. Compared to these points of failure for the paper based system, the storage of data electronically has multiple failure points.

Ask any C-suiter this simple question: "what is the Enterprise Value of the *Good Ship ERP* and the Data Sea it floats on?" You will get all kinds of answers, but most all of them will affirm the value of ERP and the data that they extract from the system. But Big ERP and "Big Data Analytics" are not the only approach one can take to running "the enterprise."

Consider the relatively low cost (and potential ROI) of a digital-free system that is setup along these lines:

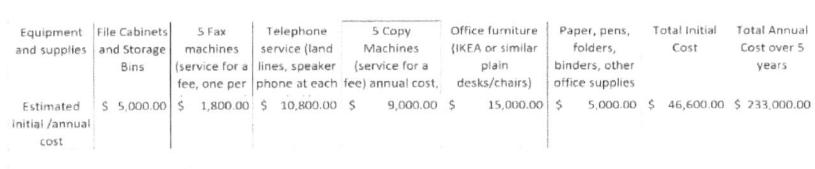

Non-digital business office

A small digression, if you allow me, about the meaning of the common phrase that describes in some vague manner what many refer to as "Cloud Computing."

As Richard Feynman correctly states, it is not really computing at all in most cases—it is an off-site filing system and data storage/retrieval system. As such, it is a needlessly expensive, elaborate, and often marginally-well supported information management system. Moreover, it is open to breach by hackers, viruses, hostage-takers. If all that were not enough, it is also at risk to an EMP strike. Feynman was absolutely correct to observe that computing is for the most part today merely apps usage, data storage, retrieval, and reporting.

In a computer heuristics lecture, Feynman described the internal part of the computer (not the input or the output portions of the whole known as a computer, but the internal "thinking" brain of the computer, the processor, as an automated electronic filing system.) The analogy is obvious: the processor in the computer is the human brain in the file clerk who manipulates the paper files to perform a task that involves the information in the file, on the card or piece of paper.

Speed and accuracy come from the computer processor, of course, not from the file clerk. The key question remains: what is really needed out of the system, and how fast is it needed? Couple this with increased storage capacity and fast retrieval and data cubes producing near-real-time transactional-based data, and you run into these basic questions:

- what does a slice from the Big Data pie mean?
- What does it "tell" the person looking at it, trying to analyze it?
- Does the data mean anything in any context now, tomorrow, ten days later, a year later?
- Is it what the person asked for?
- How is the requester to know what to ask for?[45]

---

[45] See, Feynman, https://www.youtube.com/watch?v=EKWGGDXe5MA

But what about viruses, even if you decide to fork over the bucks for one of the above service models? Consider this:

- Estimated number of computer viruses: > 50,000
- Verified number of paper viruses: < 0 (human viruses, possibly, but not likely—if handwashing is practiced as a requirement handed down from HR department 😊)

Consider the virus propagating itself in the file structure in the laptop itself or in its virtual hard drive accessed in the Cloud; contemplate the pain inflicted by the clever hacker who wants the ransom paid in bitcoin, the corruption of the database; the death of the backup thumb drive or other accessory storage devices; and then there is the hacking and virus threats that surround and seek to penetrate the Cloud itself in all of its manifestations in server farms that are connected like fragile gems on a necklace that is wound around the globe with invisible wires running up to and down from satellites in geo-stationary orbit. What potential disaster this all is by way of comparison to the disasters that you face in the paper-based system.[46]

But with foresight and the religious adherence to standard backup protocols, this risk can be mitigated to the level of being an acceptable risk, especially if the business is connected to the internet in a limited fashion and for very specific purposes. For example, a dedicated laptop is used for browsing and is not used

---

[46] For a good overview of the number of computer viruses, see: https://www.cknow.com/cms/vtutor/number-of-viruses.html; and also this for a good comparison of computer viruses: https://en.wikipedia.org/wiki/Comparison_of_computer_viruses

for any other purpose. It is breached by outside hackers, so be it. Lesson learned here is this: they are out there, they hold that one machine hostage, so what, we reimage it and go back online with a different IP address.

In this setup, then, the same workforce presented above is dedicated to running the enterprise, but they are not using paper exclusively as the medium for business transactions and information preservation and storage. They use top-end laptops interconnected via an on-premise intra-network. They are joined together within their own world of work, the office space itself.

They use their laptops (their personal "filing cabinets," as Feynman described computers in the 1980s[47]) in an off-line networked office environment, so they can share files across the office intranet with one another in a safe environment operating on a simple and stable platform; they can print from their

---

[47] Richard Feynman, in a computer heuristics lecture, described the internal part of the computer (not the input or the output portions of the whole known as a computer, but the internal "thinking" brain of the computer, the processor, as an automated electronic filing system. The analogy is obvious, the processor in the computer is the human brain in the file clerk who manipulates the paper files to perform a task that involves the information in the file, on the card or piece of paper. Speed and accuracy comes from the computer processor, of course, not from the file clerk. The question is, however, what is really needed out of the system, and how fast is it needed. Couple this with increased storage capacity and fast retrieval and data cubes producing real-time transaction based data, and you run into the basic question: what does a slice from the Big Data pie mean? What does it "tell" the person looking at it, analyzing it? What does the data mean? Is it what the person asked for, how to know what to ask for? See: https://www.youtube.com/watch?v=EKWGGDXe5MA

laptops to printers that are connected via the wireless intranet (or wired and therefore even safer from outside bad actors).

To send and receive email, they go to the email room where a single laptop is hardwired to a single DSL outlet. They use this laptop for business purposes, not for personal email. They are there to run the enterprise, to think, to cogitate, to strategize, to ponder and invent, to self-reflect, and to reflect on the business. They are not there to check for personal email, or to Tweet, or post to Facebook. They all agree to get the cell phone fix when on break, during lunch, but not during working hours. And no one violates the rule about cell phones and laptops: the two devices, one "clean and pure" and one potentially and likely malware-riddled, are never joined together. That is a cardinal hook-up sin, and they do not wish to be sinners guilty of hooking-up.

They still use dedicated faxes to send out whatever they need to send to vendors, to receive invoices from vendors, etc., so they have some paper to handle, store, and handle again when referencing vendor files. And this happens today as well in the totally online or Cloud based enterprise. Just look around the next time you are in the Cloud-based enterprise. You will see file cabinets and you will see paper. You will see Excel spreadsheets. You will see a mixture of the old and the new. It will be there, on the desk, on the table, down the hall lined with file cabinets, in the fire-rated back room full of cardboard boxes filled with invoices and sales orders. A certain mixture of the old and the new is still present in many businesses today, large and small.

Here is the estimated cost of this setup[48]:

Equipment and supplies[1]	File Cabinets and Storage Bins	Office Supplies (includes Quick Books, and other apps that are CD loaded)	5 Fax machines	Telephone service (service for a fee, one per department)	5 Copy Machines (land lines, speaker phone at each desk)	Office furniture (service for a fee) annual cost, one per department	Microsoft Surface Book 2, 256GB, Intel 1Core 5, Windows 10 Pro, one for each of the 18 employees, each @ $1500 each Book	Total cost (initial and annual combined)
Estimated initial /annual cost	$5,000 initial cost (5 year life span)	$1,000 annual / $5000 initial cost	$1,800 annual cost	$10,800 annual cost	$9,000 annual cost	$15,000 initial cost	$27,000	$74,600

Example of On-premise and Cloud Consultant Tasks, Costs, and Timeline

There are no two Enterprise situations, or solutions, or set of business needs that are identical. But they are similar enough to permit those in charge to assess which Enterprise Resource Planning (ERP) package or system best meets their operational requirements for payroll, human resources, supply replenishment, and the like. Many factors come into play when assessing ERP system cost and suitability for a given enterprise. Some standard considerations are:

- Understanding the operational complexity and routine processing requirements underlying the business;
- Assessing if the ERP packaged software will be able to accommodate the data storage and retrieval of data in an integrated manner across the standard business practices in the departments of payroll, HR, supply chain, maintenance, and so forth.
- *What drives the decision-making from the business perspective is this: will the software be functionally able to meet these various business processes in an efficient, cost-effective, secure, and largely error-free manner?*

---

[48] Estimates for initial and annual equipment costs (faxes, copies, dedicated business phone lines, etc.) based on simple queries of the largest non-relational database of all, the Internet.

- Data breach security offered by those who administer the HW and SW—IaaS, PaaS, SaaS—as well as for the strictly on-premise system setup;
- The licensing cost set by ERP vendors to use their packaged software
- Vendor and in-house staff cost to set up (or upgrade) the legacy ERP system on-premise, or to switch to IaaS, PaaS, or SaaS models
- Timeline and number of tasks needed to install, upgrade, or migrate to the desired ERP system
- Consulting costs to implement, install, upgrade, or migrate to the desired ERP system

Let's take a quick look at the kind of costs the "enterprise" faces when setting up a modern functionally rich ERP system.

First, the on-premise scenario cost applies to a hospital system that has 5,500 employees and treats 30,000 patients and 350,000 outpatients annually.[49]

Hardware Configuration Type	HW Cost	License Cost	Maintenace Cost over 5 years	TCO
Stand Alone	$ 445,000.00	$ 90,000.00	$ 45,000.00	$ 580,000.00
Integrated	$ 500,000.00	$ 30,000.00	$ 25,000.00	$ 555,000.00

For the same hospital system, this is a typical task timeline for upgrading on-premise HW and databases to run an upgraded version of the legacy ERP package:

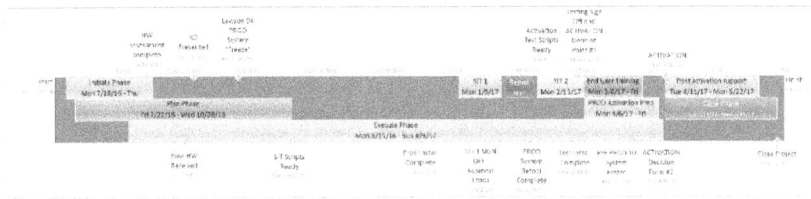

Next, the comparative TCO to keep the legacy ERP system, with upgraded HW and database setup, in house versus migrating from the

---

[49] Graphics created by author and based on prior healthcare client in CA.

legacy HW system to the Cloud. This comparison is also for the same hospital system touched on above.

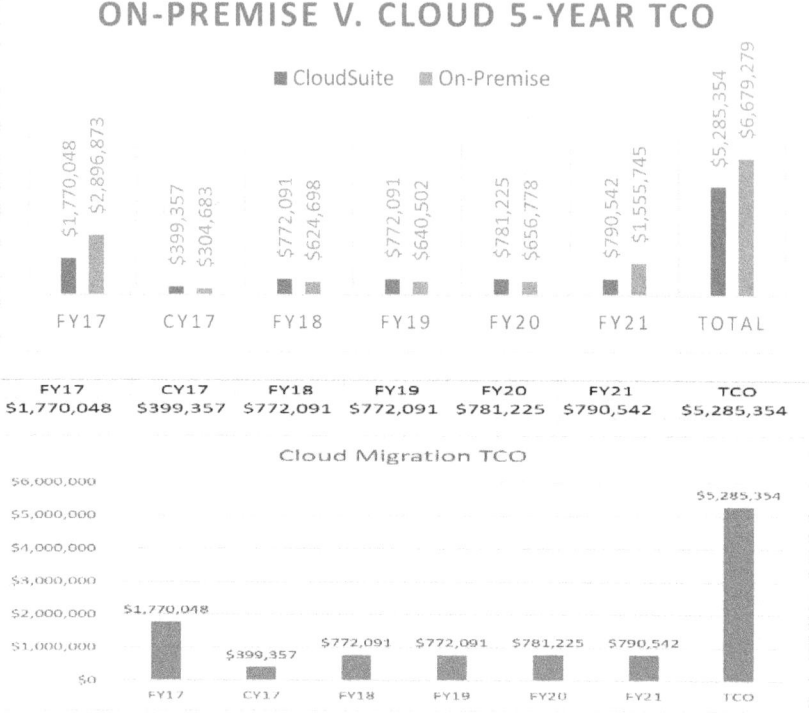

The consulting hours are also key in moving from on-premise to the Cloud, as illustrated in the following billing hours/cost graphics for the same hospital system:

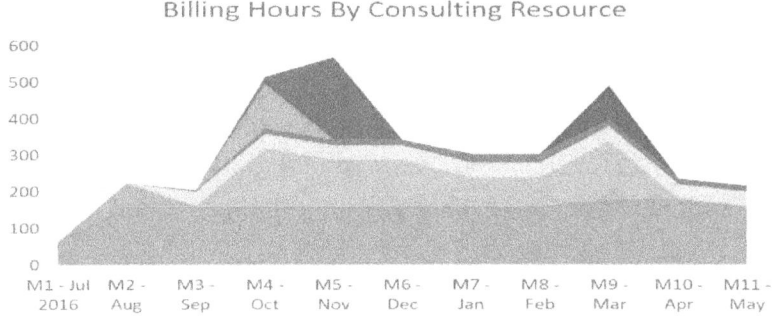

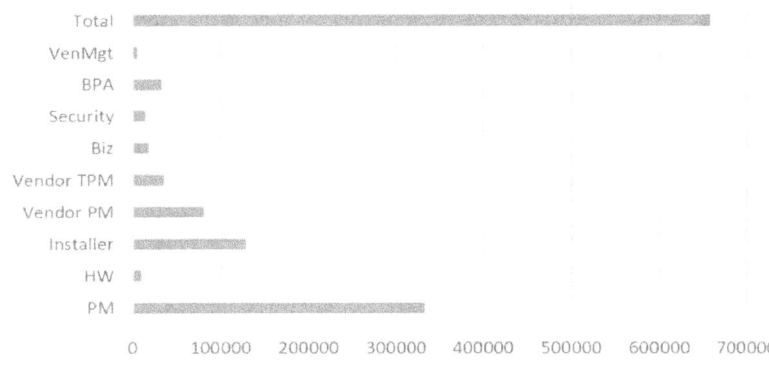

The obvious point is that the implementation, upgrade, or migration to the Cloud ERP system is an expensive proposition due to many tasks over months by many expensive consultants as well as many in-house employees. TCO is significant, to be sure.

And what about expected ROI that can be realized after all the time, effort, cost, risk, and disruption of legacy business operations, software user training requirements, and ongoing costs for system admin and support?

It is important to keep in mind that TCO focuses on actual costs (hardware, consulting billings, software, use licensing, maintenance, security, etc.). And on the other hand, ROI is thought to include benefits that will accrue to the business after the costs for the new system, the upgrade, the more sophisticated ERP package is put into place and is in use to good effect.

For example, think of TCO as being bounded by all costs associated with installing a new accounting software package that requires more hardware, more database capacity, more security, more training for finance team, etc. Contrast that TCO with anticipated ROI that will accrue down the years from the capital outlay for the new accounting system. One example would be closing the books in three to five days versus ten days in the old system. Or being able to realize better business intelligence for the CFO out of the new accounting system which enables the CFO to make decisions in the future that adds financial value and reduces financial risk to the entire enterprise.[50]

Two opposing views illustrate the ongoing discussion about ROI myth vs. reality for big ERP projects, regardless of the ERP package (SAP, ERP LN, CloudSuite, Oracle, Workday, et al.)

"... ERP benefits are by no means guaranteed. ... the risk of ERP disrupting an organization's core operations is a significant business risk. These factors are clearly areas that will affect the ROI of the investment in ERP and should be carefully managed as part of an overall ERP Benefits Realization plan."[51]

---

[50] For a brief overview of the differences between TCO and ROI, see: https://www.cio.com/article/2436828/metrics/tco-versus-roi.html

[51] See, https://www.panorama-consulting.com/erp-benefits-myth-or-reality/

And, on the other hand, there are proponents of the opposite view who see little chance of not realizing significant ROI when measuring these parameters:

- *"Reduced level of inventory through improved planning and control.*
- *Improved production efficiency which minimizes shortages and interruptions.*
- *Reduced materials cost through improved procurement and payment protocols.*
- *Reduced labor cost through better allocation of staff and reduced overtime.*
- *Increased sales revenue, driven by better managed customer relationships.*
- *Increased gross margin percentage.*
- *Reduced administrative costs.*
- *Reduced regulatory compliance costs.*

And there are plenty of other achievable benefits, both tangible and intangible. Properly implemented and managed, ERP can be a significant driver of ROI. For the CFO, the first order of business is to determine the desired ERP benefits so that the process can be well-measured."[52]

Well, what is next on your agenda?

27 radical suggestions for the ("WOKE") CEOs, CFOs, CTOs, CDOs, and their Boards of Directors

Options to the entire Cloud, Big Data, AI, Machine Learning cluster think *must be radical ones in nature* or they will merely be

---

[52] See, http://www.compudata.com/calculating-roi-what-the-cfo-needs-to-know-about-erp/

a version of the current rush to be "all in" for . . . (fill in the blank).

1. Hire a qualified "Enterprise Techno-transformation Consultant" to help plan and schedule the radical use of technology to run the enterprise
2. Design the plan, the process, and the schedule to radically transform the way and extent to which the Enterprise uses Big ERP and Big Data to run the business
3. Put IT/IS department and its CIO/CTO leadership on notice that its role in the enterprise will be changing; invite willing participation, and if resistance is evident, let them go
4. Devise the plan, work the plan, run a pilot program, measure results, make corrections and adjustments, then phase in the new system across the enterprise—no big bang permitted
5. Engage legal to give notice to terminate all existing contracts with Cloud, PaaS, SaaS, AI, et al. vendors
6. Invest in human intelligence rather than AI because AI just might prove to be irreparably dumbing-down for the employees (and it might quite possibly be anthropomorphic suicide to do otherwise)
7. Replace IT staff as needed with intelligent cross-functional employees who can add value to the enterprise beyond what information technology "experts" can contribute

8. Ignore the empty rhetoric and half-baked technobabble of Big ERP and Big Data sales engineers who push all versions of PaaS, IaaS, SaaS, IoT, AI, Machine Learning
9. Do not use the internet in any way to access enterprise business apps and data
10. Use simple off-the-shelf (OTS) technology and intelligent thinking employees to run the enterprise
11. Setup your own "business continuity/data recovery" system that is nowhere near the Cloud or internet
12. Use only as much technology as needed to run the business, and then figure out how to use even less technology to run the business
13. Setup hard-wired non-internet connected intranets (LAN/WAN, but no internal Wi-Fi)
14. Prohibit accessing the internet from any digital device inside the workplace
15. Prohibit connecting any employee owned digital device (cell phone, thumb drive, etc.) to the LAN/WAN
16. Prohibit use of cell phones while at work except when on breaks, at lunch, etc.
17. Study and understand what worked well, how, and why in the paper-based ERP enterprise before the advent of the computer and digitized paper office forms were turned into integrated apps
18. Keep the tool-set simple, low-tech, proven, reliable, low-cost, and easily replaced off the shelf (re: laptops, multi-function printers, copiers, fax machines from Office Max, Best Buy, etc.)

19. Keep all data and all business applications/tools on premise
20. Educate everyone on the contextual meaning of data, and how to understand its uses, limits, and pitfalls
21. Hire high-IQ staff who will be expected to question, think, and contribute creatively to the enterprise
22. Run payroll in house using OTS software (AHC permitted via dedicated internet connected and LAN/WAN isolated laptop)
23. Send everyone in Finance to an in-house "Excel College" and test them to demonstrate their high-level of mastery of all things Excel
24. Educate everyone in Finance, HR, Supply Chain, and Payroll in how to use Access to make their own (networked) relational databases
25. Rigorously examine all business processes and practices, and re-engineer them as needed to improve efficiency, cross-discipline collaboration of ideas, and sharing of data, information, and knowledge
26. Identify the best sources of commercially available custom business process apps forms, then teach the business users how to customize them to meet their own business process needs
27. Send everyone in Finance, HR, Supply Chain Management, IT, and the C-Suite to "Data College" so they understand what data is, how to use it, how not to use it, and what to create, use, and how to understand

reports based on data mined from the enterprise's data sources

34 thought points to ponder when putting your feet are up on your desk

1. Significant achievements pre-electronic age of computer
2. Brainpower and hands-on training, say, show, do, repeat
3. Transition to computers—tech revolutions and implications across the workforce
4. Shift was to SW, the accessible brainpower, but only somewhat, dumbing down, SD implications
5. ERP and activity models: paper, electronic on site, ASP, Cloud, hybrid
6. Cost comparisons, hacking, viruses, security, offshore support models, quality control
7. Just fill out the forms on the screen (like before, fill out the forms on your desk)
8. Relational database, forms on screen inter-connected via the data flows
9. The note, the memo, the report, the dashboard
10. So much data, and limited ability to make sense of it
11. Presenting data, from the simple to the complex, and the presentation's impact on understanding what is being presented
12. The limits of acting on what data indicates (anomalies, one-time events, spikes, trends, patterns, randomness)
13. Data is what was, is, could be, but not what must be
14. What offsets ROI, the IRR in Cloud? In AI?

15. Minimize risk, being it all inhouse, empower Human IT/IS
16. Buy only what is needed when needed
17. Cloud means thin client base and many hidden negatives
18. Educate in data assessment in all scenarios
19. Evolving tech, evolving work force, fall out, implications are what
20. Radical change for good of business and workers (paradigm shift)
21. People before technology
22. Paper system worked then—why not now
23. Limited intranet, file sharing, networking to printers, faxes, landlines
24. No standing IT staff, outsource intranet design, build out, support (Xerox printer support model)
25. Off the shelf software, or design own forms, go for customization to extent needed
26. No Cloud SaaS models of any kind
27. No internet permitted into the intranet
28. No cell phones at work
29. Flip the pyramid, like Ford did with line supervisors, leads, foremen, ordinary line workers
30. Emphasize reading, collaboration, the office library, where FTEs and info finders help locate and print material/save for internal reading, sharing, discussion
31. Stress decision making, thinking, critical analysis, writing skills, understanding data, graphs, etc.

32. Invest in education of workforce onsite (to support and bolster ability to engage in business analytics, line level responsibility, grant decision making authority)
33. What next, and why should anyone care?
34. AI and Machine Learning: Do the potential benefits outweigh the potential cost and risk for the workforce?"

Closing Thoughts: To Give Way to the Borg, or to Maintain Human Supremacy?

Here is my take on the foregoing excursion into the tensions (that I believe are extremely important) between the two realms: Human Intelligence (HI) and Machine Intelligence (MI). Or, put another way, and more to the bigger point: what are the implications associated with the human/spiritual and the machine/data points of intersection, and, inevitably, the "intercourse" between the two realms?

What follows is a representative series of images that illustrate man's interest (compulsion?) in interacting with machine/data programmed by humans to interact with humans—whether in the work place, at the chess board, or in the privacy of the bedroom. The moral and ethical implications are manifold, and while of importance, are best addressed by trained and skilled moralists, ethicists, and philosophers.

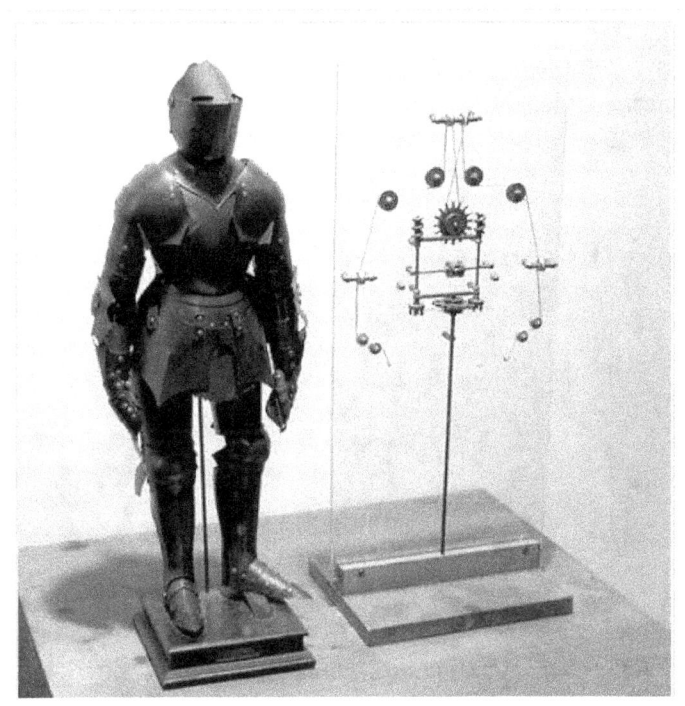

Leonardo's robot, circa 1495

Charles Babbage (1791-1871) English polymath, created the idea of a digital programmable computer. His machine was named the "Analytical Engine." [53]

Ada Lovelace (1815-1852) creator of an algorithm for Charles Babbage's Analytical Engine. Acknowledged as the "first programmer."[54]

---

[53] See, https://en.wikipedia.org/wiki/Charles_Babbage
[54] See, https://en.wikipedia.org/wiki/Ada_Lovelace

Above is a picture of Alan Turing (1912-1954).[55]

---

[55] See, https://en.wikipedia.org/wiki/Alan_Turing

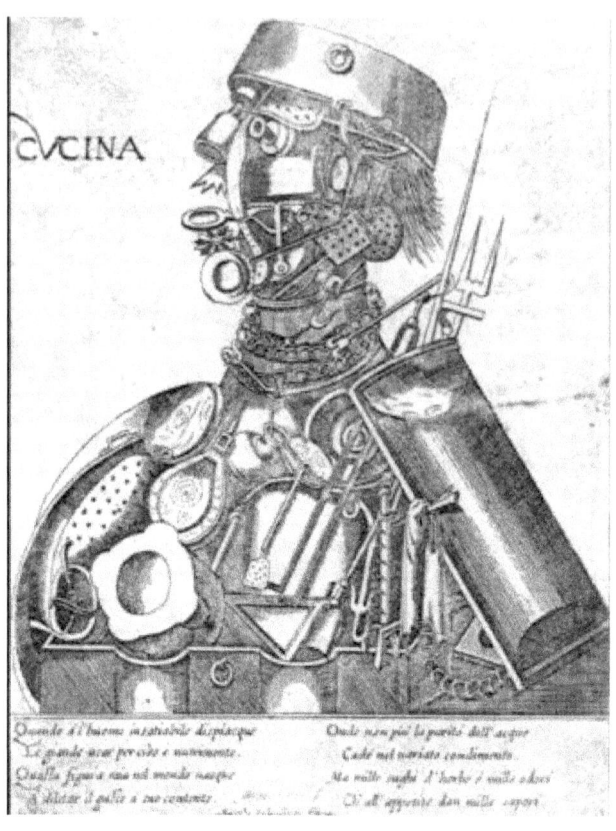

Image of a Cyborg by an unknown engraver.[56]

---

[56] See, https://en.wikipedia.org/wiki/Cyborg

John von Neumann (1903-1957)[57]

---

[57] See, https://en.wikipedia.org/wiki/John_von_Neumann

Android (human like robot) showing internal wiring, etc.[58]

---

[58] See, https://en.wikipedia.org/wiki/Android_(robot)

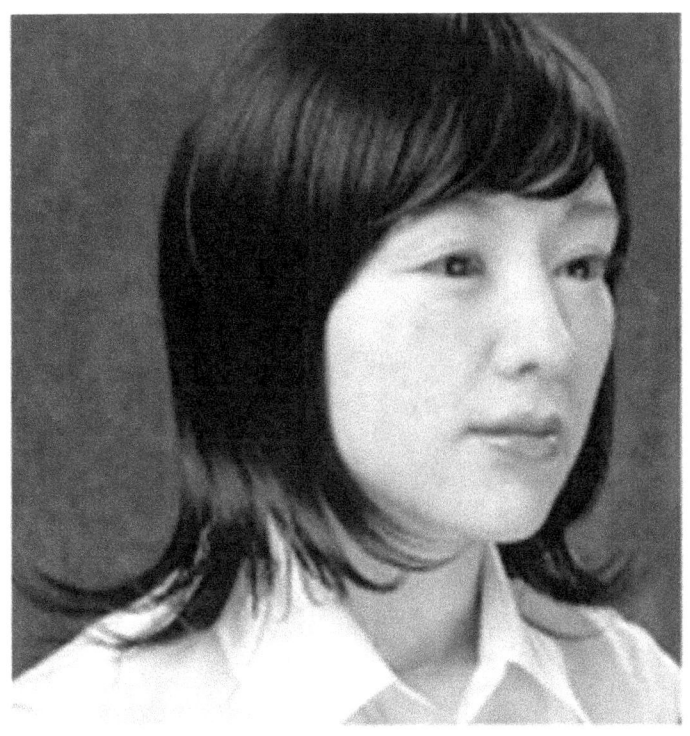

Picture of a Japanese-developed android who was programmed and engineered to "sing."[59]

---

[59] This is a photograph of EveR-2, a female android developed by the Korea Institute of Industrial Technology and demonstrated to the public in October 2006. It is 165cm tall and weighs 60kg. 18 October 2006. Source: http://news.naver.com/main/read.nhn?mode=LSD&mid=sec&sid1=102&oid=020&aid=0000371339
Author: Korea Institute of Industrial Technology (한국생산기술연구원)

Deep Blue, IBM's chess machine[60]

---

[60] https://en.wikipedia.org/wiki/Deep_Blue_(chess_computer)

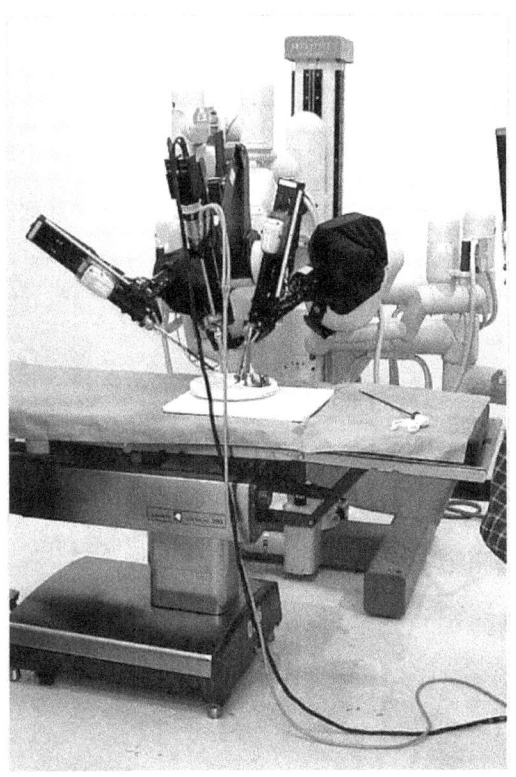

Robot-assisted surgery[61]

---

[61] See, https://en.wikipedia.org/wiki/Robot-assisted_surgery

An industrial robot used in manufacturing[62]

---

[62] See, https://en.wikipedia.org/wiki/Industrial_robot

There is evidence of human interest in sex robots, e.g., in Roman mythology.[63]

Today's customizable android (a "sex doll") designed for sale to the buying public who want them for sexual interaction.[64]

---

[63] See, https://qz.com/822789/ancient-roman-mythology-shows-an-obsession-with-sex-robots-thats-lasted-thousands-of-years/

[64] See, https://www.maxim.com/gear/new-customizable-sex-doll-2018-1

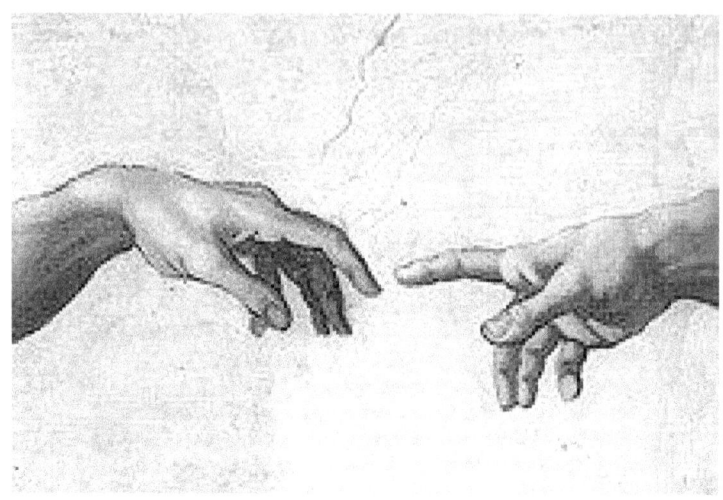

Above Michelangelo's c. 1500s depiction on the ceiling of the Sistine Chapel of God giving life to Adam[65]

First, let us look at and consider the contrapuntal implications that should be self-evident in the above series of images that end with Michelangelo's famous rendering of God giving Adam, the proto-human—the life force that Adam would then pass on to all future humans.

. Here are some of the obvious implications that I want to discuss in brief:

- The manifestation of the human intellect can be assessed as encompassing:
    - Abstract reasoning, as in: philosophy, metaphysics, mathematics, linguistics, software.
    - Applied reasoning, as in: fire, hand tools, agriculture, electricity, machines, airplanes, computers, AI, robotics

---

[65] See, https://en.wikipedia.org/wiki/Gallery_of_Sistine_Chapel_ceiling

- The manifestation of the creative human spirit can be assessed as encompassing:
    - Creative arts, as in: music, painting, dance, fiction, cinema, plays
    - Spiritual beliefs and practices, as in: paganism, the world's religions and practices)

In a recent interview with *Breitbart News Daily*, George Gilder, a "who is known as a "futurist," has an interesting take on the "contrapuntal" human manifestations touched on above. About Google and other AI firms flourishing in Silicon Valley, Gilder observes: "When you don't believe in God, it's not that you believe in nothing, it's that you'll believe in anything. . .. And Silicon Valley needs a religious vision. And it's religious vision is that its artificial intelligence can transcend human minds."[66]

Gilder's statement touches on the notion that one product of the human intellect—in his view, AI—has supplanted the panoply of deities that are found in the world's organized religions in the 21st Century. Put another way, he invites one to consider the implications of placing AI at the center of one's secular religiosity, elevating it to the point that it replaces the notion of deity with the secular God AI.

Thus, the disparity between Michelangelo's depiction of God transmitting from himself into Adam the human life force. One can contrast this concept and belief central to many of the world's major religions (and the theology behind them) to AI, the software and electro-mechanical engineering underlying the reality of a human engaging in romantic and/or sexual

---

[66] See, https://www.breitbart.com/tech/2018/08/17/george-gilder-google-repeats-marxs-errors-is-usurping-human-minds/

intercourse with a life-like, programmable "sex doll" or android designed to engage in sexual intercourse with humans.

So, am I suggesting that the Captains of Industry should have been, or should today be, a new Caste of High Priests who are all about ensuring that AI never becomes a reality? Or that today's CIOs/CTOs and CEO possess if not formal degrees and training in morality, ethics, and the history and role of religion in the affairs of mankind?

Of course not. That will never happen, we all know that. However, I am recommending that the purpose and dignity of human endeavor in the workplace be given due consideration by the executives in charge of "business processes." That they pay as much attention to the following as they do to the bottom line:

- the role of the worker in a world ever-dominated by machinery, AI, data, computers
- the meaningfulness, or lack of same, in the work they perform
- the dignity, or lack of same, in the work they perform
- the satisfaction, or lack of same, in the "work" they perform based on their individual intellects and collaborative group mental abilities

Much of what the IPC/ATAP scenario presented earlier in this lecture is all about—in case you forgot already, I am referring to Jim, our young MIT grad being promoted into the IPC/ATAP—addresses in many respects the thrust of what the futurist Gilder is calling to our attention.

In an article in *Wired*, "God is the Machine," the author traces the development of a line of thinking that runs something like this in my attempt to paraphrase it:

Everything in the universe--whether corporeal or incorporeal--is essentially reducible to information, or to 1s and 0s. In short, the universe is information, is 1s and 0s, is the ultimate computational machine, is the ultimate digital computer, is God—if one wants to put a theological dimension into the mix.

Here is the essence of the article, and I quote this time:

"Weaving together the esoteric teachings of quantum physics with the latest theories in computer science, pioneering digital thinkers are outlining a way of understanding all of physics as a form of computation. . ... From this perspective, computation seems almost a theological process. It takes as its fodder the primeval choice between yes or no, the fundamental state of 1 or 0. After stripping away all externalities, all material embellishments, what remains is the purest state of existence: here/not here. Am/not am. In the Old Testament, when Moses asks the Creator, "Who are you?" the being says, in effect, "Am." One bit. One almighty bit. Yes. One. Exist. It is the simplest statement possible."[67]

While, as a scientist I find such speculation of interest, as a poet and philosopher I find it lacking. It is ultimately a dry, empty, wanting explanation of "everything."

Why I find it lacking, I trust you can figure that out for yourself, having sat through this lengthy lecture. If you cannot, perhaps you and I should have selected different 1s and 0s, and in doing so, we would have had GOD himself make it possible for us to avoid this lecture and the man who delivered it.

---

[67] See, https://www.wired.com/2002/12/holytech/

Encouraging Words

I encourage each of you, the learned members of this (reading) audience, to do the following at a bare minimum when you return to your well-appointed executive suites:

1. assemble all the pertinent facts for each likely and not-so-likely scenario (ask your vendors for their fact-based recommendations--but do your own research without fail
2. be sure to include all possible scenarios (think outside the cloud, outside the data, outside the capital and non-capital cost parameters)
3. assess, discuss, and examine all the facts at hand in a thoroughly impartial manner
4. use your intellect when making your decisions on which path forward will best meet your "Enterprise" needs (following your "gut" will only lead you to the lavatory)
5. assemble your findings into one report that includes the "technical trade-off case," the "business case," the "social-system user case," and of course "a human spiritual case"
6. present your internal findings to your entire executive and business leadership team and ask them to respond in all candor with their assessment of your assessments and findings; do the same with your vendors and ask them to challenge your facts, assumptions, and value judgments as they apply to your individual work environment and the people who work in it)
7. Weigh all factors again and make the most intelligent final decision you can, then get the buy in from

"informed" executives and workers alike for the proposed course of action.

Another final word

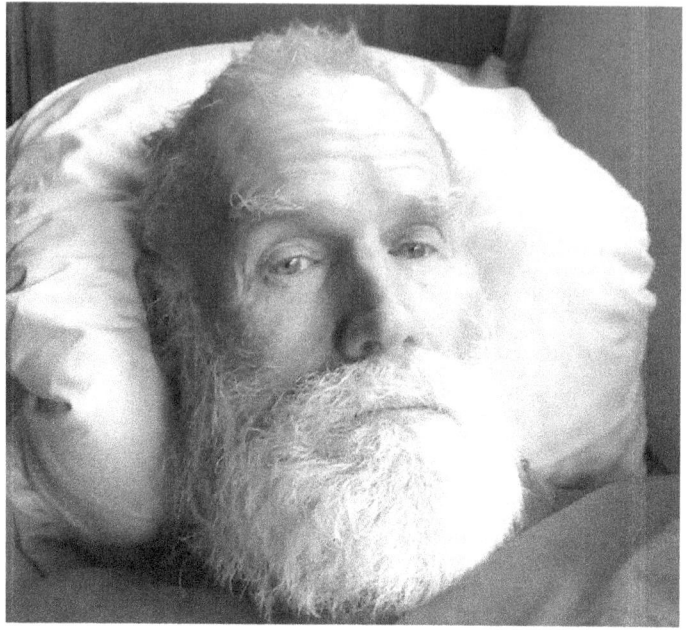

The Good Doctor at rest after delivering the C^5 Lecture

In conclusion, I could say that I wish you the "best of luck" with your chosen path as you wrestle with your future choices and all the variables facing you as you determine your future in the workplace. But we all know it takes sound navigational skills and not luck to reach the safe harbor that lies beyond the cloud-obscured horizon.

This assumes, of course, that in the affairs of mice and men, there is such a thing as a "safe harbor" in the sea of data about us, and soon, in us as well.

Post-lecture comments

Here are some comments overheard from the mouths of those who fall into one of the groups below. Enjoy.

CIO/CDO/CTO comments

"What the X##@@VV&&&%%$!!!!!!!!!!!!!!!!!!!!!!!!!!!!!!!"

"Who the hell does this guy think he is? And what crazy kind of a format is this so-called LECTURE, anyway?"

"I am going to request my money back, and if I could, my time back. God knows I deserve both, even though the latter might be hard to arrange."

"A little Cloud knowledge really is a dangerous thing. And he proves it in Spades! I am will keep a sharp eye out for him and block any onsite visits, you can count on that."

"What is all this ATAP claptrap? Pie in the sky, if you ask me. And anyone can dredge up stats to make any case one wants, and he has done a lot of selective dredging."

"Wake me when this abomination is over."

"I don't know if he is ignorant, stubborn, well-meaning, or just being provocative to earn a buck and bolster his credentials as a nay-sayer. I am guessing it's a bit of everything."

"He does not know the first thing about the use-value of the Cloud, let alone of Big Data when properly captured, stored, retrieved, and interpreted."

"Ultimate computer is same as the entire universe. Makes no sense at all, because there is no Cloud in outer space as far as I know.

CEO comments

"I've got to Google Feynman on data storage and ask others on the team what they think."

"Bet that many in the audience have thought about some version of what he called the ATAP but dismissed it out of hand as being too impossible. But I am going to take a hard look all the same."

"What I got so far is, hey, open your mind and let the light of other perspectives shine in. Always useful, a healthy dose of open-mindedness and skepticism, especially in today's world of IT group think."

"I think I will invite this guy to come onsite, and then if that goes well, maybe ask him to speak to the Board. We need to consider all perspectives and options, no matter how unorthodox, before we commit to spending millions on the new world-wide IT system the CTO and vendor are recommending."

"I doubt much will come of this lecture for most in the audience, but I intend to re-think our planned use of AI to mine Big Data in the Cloud."

"I can't wait to ask my CIO what he thinks of low-tech in the office. It will be very informative."

"I appreciate him challenging the idea that transforming the enterprise via software is self-evidently a good thing and is therefore out of bounds for the doubting executive. For CEOs to not question everything is a kind of hubris that is hard to justify when so much depends on our sound decisions."

ERP Vendor Comments

(All vendor comments overheard were deemed to be so profanity-laced that I have decided they should not be printed. This decision was made not so much out of respect for the genteel sensibilities of the informed American reading public, as it was to my adherence to the proposition that one should not aid and abet the end-game of hate speech by reproducing any of it in any form.)

www.ingramcontent.com/pod-product-compliance
Lightning Source LLC
Chambersburg PA
CBHW071034240526
45469CB00006BD/2202